Students Taking Charge

Inside the Learner-Active, Technology-Infused Classroom

Nancy Sulla

Routledge
Taylor & Francis Group

LONDON AND NEW YORK

First published 2011 by Eye on Education

Published 2013 by Routledge
2 Park Square, Milton Park, Abingdon, Oxon OX14 4RN
711 Third Avenue, New York, NY, 10017, USA

Routledge is an imprint of the Taylor & Francis Group, an informa business

Library of Congress Cataloging-in-Publication Data
Sulla, Nancy.
   Students taking charge : inside the learner-active, technology-infused classroom /
   by Nancy Sulla.
      p. cm.
   ISBN 978-1-59667-185-0
   1. Student-centered learning. 2. Active learning. 3. Effective teaching.
   4. Classroom environment. I. Title.
   LB1027.23.S85 2011
   371.39'4—dc22

                                                                    2011008166

ISBN 13: 978-1-59667-185-0 (pbk)

Designer and Compositor: Richard Adin, Freelance Editorial Services
Cover Designer: David Strauss

Also Available from EYE ON EDUCATION

Battling Boredom:
99 Strategies to Spark Student Engagement
Bryan Harris

Helping Students Motivate Themselves:
Practical Answers to Classroom Challenges
Larry Ferlazzo

ENGAGING Teens in Their Own Learning:
8 Keys to Student Success
Paul J. Vermette

The Passion-Driven Classroom:
A Framework for Teaching & Learning
Angela Maiers and Amy Sandvold

Classroom Motivation from A to Z:
How to Engage Your Students in Learning
Barbara R. Blackburn

Rigor is NOT a Four-Letter Word
Barbara R. Blackburn

Differentiated Instruction Using Technology:
A Guide for Middle and High School Teachers
Amy Benjamin

Getting the Most Out of Your Interactive Whiteboard:
A Practical Guide
Amy Buttner

How the Best Teachers Differentiate Instruction
Elizabeth Breaux and Monique B. Magee

Wikis for School Leaders:
Using Technology to Improve Communication and Collaboration
Stephanie D. Sandifer

Differentiated Instruction for K-8 Math & Science:
Ideas, Activities, and Lesson Plans
Mary Hamm and Dennis Adams

What Do You Say When...?
Best Practice Language for Improving Student Behavior
Hal Holloman and Peggy H. Yates

Dedication

To God, who always has a great plan for my days, and
Team IDE—an amazing group of people with whom I have
had the pleasure of working across the years and who,
collaboratively, innovate better than any team I know.

Meet the Author

Nancy Sulla is the founder and President of IDE Corp. (Innovative Designs for Education), an educational consulting company specializing in instructional and organizational design. She holds a B.A. in Education from Fairleigh Dickinson University, an M.A. in computer science from Montclair State University, and an Ed.D. in Educational Administration from Fordham University. Her diverse background includes teaching at the elementary, middle school, high school, and college levels; working as a computer programmer and systems analyst; and leading teachers as a district administrator prior to launching IDE Corp. Her consulting work ranges from focused topics such as problem-based learning, web tools, and differentiation to the more systems-based work of designing Small Learning Communities and redesigning schools.

Free Downloads

Many of the tools discussed and displayed in this book are also available on the Routledge website as Adobe Acrobat files. Permission has been granted to purchasers of this book to download these tools and print them.

You can access these downloads by visiting www.routledge.com/9781596671850 and clicking on the Free Downloads tab.

Index of Free Downloads

Contents

Introduction

Passion lies at the intersection of a dream and success. Those who are passionate about their craft typically have a dream of what can be, and have had glimpses of that dream in small pockets of success along the way. That combination fuels a desire to keep moving forward, regardless of personal sacrifice, fully believing that this is the road on which they are meant to travel.

The field of education is graced with many passionate teachers—those who believe that all students can learn and are fueled by those moments when students perform beyond their expectations. The Greek philosopher Heraclitus said that you can never step in the same river twice, because the river is constantly changing. So it is with the classroom. Each day brings newness: students are constantly changing, growing, and learning; passionate teachers are continually honing their craft; society possesses a momentum that repeatedly presents new challenges for schools.

Passionate teachers see beyond the barriers; they know there is a better way to prepare young people for their future and to unleash in them all the potential they possess. They explore new ways of approaching teaching and learning, and, fueled by isolated and sometimes small encounters with success, they forge ahead. I have no doubt that the relentless pursuit of instructional innovation by the passionate few will overcome the barriers of resistance and create innovative, adaptive learning environments that will both serve and form society in ways beyond our current imagination.

My own passion for pursuing instructional and organizational innovation in schools is fueled by the wonderful stories I've collected over the years from my own teaching; from my encounters with passionate teachers who have taken my vision and turned it into reality; and from my collaboration with the dedicated, creative, and innovative people with whom I've had the pleasure to work at IDE Corp.

My vision for the *Learner-Active, Technology-Infused Classroom* was inspired by many moments throughout my life. When I was ten, I began running a summer school program for the neighborhood children; by the time I was twelve, I was charging fees and holding graduation ceremonies for parents. In some ways, it was a one-room schoolhouse; I had neighborhood children of all ages anxious to come to my school for the three days a week it was open, including those who were gifted, those with learning difficulties, and a child with cerebral palsy. To meet their needs, I assigned varying work and spent a lot of my time working in small groups and with individual students. I still look back in amazement that the neighborhood kids hated to miss a day of summer school, given that we truly worked the entire time! One bright and talented young man had been attending my school since age three. When his mom had her first parent–teacher conference, his teacher pointed out how far ahead he was from his peers, no doubt because of the private school he was attending. Today, the young man is a judge, and I like to think his early experiences in "school" helped to fuel his own passion for his craft.

An early experience in my teaching career inspired me to solidify my vision and articulate it so that others could join my quest for the ultimate learning environment. It was the late seventies, my second year in teaching and first year teaching middle school. I was assigned the lower-level math students who had repeatedly failed the state tests. I remember starting class asking my eighth graders to take out their books, only to find that few brought them. Paper? Pencil? My efforts to recreate the traditions experienced in my own schooling seemed futile. One day, I asked my students to simply show up for class the next day—no books, no paper, no pencils. They all complied. I had pushed back the desks and arranged the chairs in a circle. I explained that I wanted to keep my job and they needed to learn math, and I asked them for the solution to my dilemma. My students pointed out that math instruction was boring and they didn't see the point. I suggested that perhaps I could design projects that would make the learning more meaningful; they agreed to give it a try.

I don't remember the first project I designed, nor the entire complement, but I do recall a few. We created scale drawings of birdhouses to build; we used paper plates to create polyhedra disco balls (it was, after all, the seventies). In those days, teachers could take their students out to play kickball on a nice day. My students would head out with clipboards to track the progress of the game; once inside, they would run the statistics on the game and analyze it in light of previous games. When the state tests arrived, my students did quite well, with almost all of them passing. I remember my principal asking me what I did; I didn't know. He persisted and pointed out that my students performed particularly well on percentages, but I simply shrugged my shoulders and admitted I hadn't gotten to that chapter yet.

Years later, I realized what had happened. I had designed higher-order problems for my students to solve, and then provided them with the resources and support they needed to learn. I realized, too, that the problems did not encompass only the skills in a single chapter of the textbook; they spanned many chapters. I would venture to say we worked with percentages, for example, in most of the problems. I saw the power of students learning from a *felt need* in an authentic context, and that year and the successes my teaching style yielded never left me.

It was, however, the invention of the desktop computer and its arrival in schools that further fueled my vision for the classroom. Teachers are faced with a classroom of students with varying needs and interests; computers provide them with a wealth of opportunities to help students learn. In the early eighties, I was a district-level administrator, when I decided to make "an offer to innovate" to a couple of teachers. Alysse Daches and Cyndie Bach taught fourth and fifth grade, respectively. They were both among the daring few who purchased desktop computers for their homes. I asked how they would like to have five desktop computers for their classrooms, and they jumped at the chance. Over the course of the next few months, I saw a new vision for the classroom spring to life. On one visit they told me they felt guilty that the computers sat vacant while they were teaching lessons; I suggested that perhaps they could reduce the number of whole-class lessons in favor of other means of providing instruction. On another visit they told me how challenging it was for the children to push together desks of all different sizes and attempt to work collaboratively. I replaced the desks with 42-inch-round tables. Structure by structure, strategy by strategy, my vision for instruction took shape. More than twenty years later, with myriad classroom teachers implementing the *Learner-Active, Technology-Infused Classroom*, I wrote this book to capture the essence of this classroom to share with passionate teachers everywhere.

The book is intended to be a guide to designing an Authentic Learning Unit, which is at the core of the *Learner-Active, Technology-Infused Classroom*, and the structures and strategies to support its implementation. I believe it's best if you pause after each chapter and spend some time designing the various components of the unit. The early chapters delve into designing an appropriate core problem for students to solve and the analytic rubric to provide them with clearly articulated expectations. Chapter 4 introduces the notion of "participatory structures," or ways in which students participate in the learning process. Chapter 5 addresses differentiation techniques. Although much is written about lesson-level differentiation, this chapter also addresses unit-level differentiation and classroom-level differentiation. Chapter 6 offers a variety of structures and strategies for creating an environment in which students take responsibility for the own learning and thus engage more fully in the learning process. Chapter 7 offers a look at facilitating learning in this environment. Chapter 8 addresses physical classroom design, which will prove to be more useful for those who have more control over their physical classroom space than for those who do not. The ten principles of the *Learner-Active, Technology-Infused Classroom* are woven throughout and then addressed more fully in the final chapter.

I hope this book helps to fuel your passion and provide you with many ideas for innovatively designing your classroom.

1

The Big Picture for Your Instructional Design Journey

Shifting Mindsets

Imagine a learning environment in which students pose questions and actively seek answers. They decide how they will use their time; take charge of setting and achieving goals; and work individually to build skills and collaboratively develop solutions to real-world problems. Computer technology is used throughout the day, seamlessly, as students and teachers need it—from handheld devices to laptops to interactive whiteboards. Students walk to a flat-screen monitor on the wall and talk to students in another part of the world. Teachers move around the room, sitting with students who share their accomplishments, asking probing questions and gathering assessment data that will shape tomorrow's instructional plans. You hear students talking about content; their vocabulary is sophisticated for their grade level; their thinking processes are evident through their discussions and reflections. They are intent on the task at hand, yet not everyone is working on the same thing at the same time. No one is off task; no one is misbehaving. Every now and then you hear a cheer or a student exclaim, "I got it!" as they excitedly dive into the next phase of a project. They pack up certain activities and move on to others without the prompting of the teacher. No one watches the clock; no one wants to leave. This is a snapshot of the *Learner-Active, Technology-Infused Classroom*. Students in this classroom take learning seriously and pursue it vigorously. Teachers in this classroom masterfully craft learning experiences that emanate from authentic problem situations; they facilitate learning, ensuring that each student achieves at the highest level. Parents are partners in the learning process, often via the Internet, working with teachers and students as one cohesive unit to ensure that the students are given the best foundation possible for the rest of their lives.

You may recognize aspects of your own classroom or those of your colleagues. Pockets of innovation exist in schools; it's time to stop celebrating pockets of change, incremental improvements, and isolated innovative teachers. It's time to take bold moves to secure the future of our students and the world.

The Role of Schooling

Schools both serve and form society. They serve society by building in their students the skills, concepts, and information needed to thrive in today's world. When the sundial gave way to the analog clock, people needed new skills. When the slide rule gave way to the calculator, school curriculum changed. The school community must continually consider changes in society, particularly technological changes, and ensure that the curriculum is designed to shape successful world citizens.

In addition to critical subject-area content mastery, students need to build skills in creativity, innovation, critical thinking, problem solving, communication, collaboration, information literacy, technological literacy, initiative, self-direction, socializing, cross-cultural engagement, productivity, leadership, flexibility, adaptability, accountability, and responsibility. How do you build "ility?" Most of these skills cannot be approached as a subject. A student cannot take a class in flexibility and adaptability. These skills that fall outside of subject-area content are acquired based on *how* teachers teach more than *what* they teach.

If schools serve society by *what* they teach, then they form society by *how* they teach. Schools that place a great emphasis on individual competition develop citizens that are well-suited for that, but may not be as able or willing to work collaboratively. Schools that place a great emphasis on project management, time management, and resourcefulness develop citizens that are better prepared to lead self-reliant, productive lives. This is a connection that schools often fail to realize, and it is why teachers and administrators must very carefully develop an ongoing, purposeful, instructional design plan that not only considers the written curriculum—the why—but also directs the teaching and learning process in the classroom—the how.

Moving Beyond "It's Always Been That Way"

Consider this anecdote I once heard. A mother is cooking a ham dinner. She cuts off the end of the ham, places the larger piece in the pan, and begins to roast it. Her young daughter says, "Mommy, why do you cut off the end of the ham?" Mom responds, "You know, I'm not sure but my mother always did that. Go ask grandma." The young girl goes into the living room and asks her grandmother the same question. The response is, "I don't know; my mom did that so I did too," and she turned to her great-grandmother and asked why. The elderly woman responded, "Well, otherwise it wouldn't fit in my roasting pan!"

What a wonderful anecdote for the ills of perpetuating the dominant paradigm of schooling. Teachers always stood in the front of the room when I was in school, so that must be where you stand. We always had textbooks, so they must be a necessary part of school. We've always had students write and solve problems on the board, so that must a necessary component of mathematics instruction. It's time to think through what schooling looks like and make some significant adjustments to past practices. That's not to say you discard everything you currently do. Rather, you keep what works and make some adjustments. The important thing is to keep your mind continually open to change and be willing to shift some of your beliefs as to what the teaching and learning process could look like.

Shifting your belief system is not an easy process; it requires unlearning some of what you've learned in the past. Authors Ron Heifetz and Marty Linksy (2002) distinguish between technical and adaptive change. Technical change focuses on implementing known solutions to problems. For example, if students are not performing up to your desired level, you might use a rubric to offer them clearly articulated expectations. You learn how to use a rubric, implement its use, and teach others. That's technical change, which is the focus of most professional development and college courses today in the field of education. Adaptive change focuses on developing solutions to problems for which none yet exists. Designing classrooms to meet a new, emerging generation of learners is a problem for which there can be no available solution, given that students and society are continually changing. Adaptive change requires a change in one's belief system.

Three Critical Goals

Teachers should have at their core three critical goals for instructional design: engage students in learning; build greater responsibility for student learning; and increase academic rigor.

Engaged Learners

Busy students are not necessarily engaged students, nor are seemingly happy students who are working in groups. Although "hands-on" activities are wonderful, what you truly want are "minds-on" activities. If you assume students are engaged in learning, take a closer look to see if what they are doing is directly related to academically rigorous content and if they are thinking deeply about that content. Suppose third-grade students are learning about the food chain. Consider the following scenarios as we peek into three classrooms:

- Students are locating information on the food chain from books and the Internet and creating charts to demonstrate their understanding of the food chain.

- Students are designing a computer presentation on the food chain and are working on adding sounds and transitions to make it more exciting.

- Students are developing a presentation that considers "what if" a member of the food chain were to become extinct, under what conditions that might happen, and how that would affect the rest of the food chain.

Although all three scenarios cover the content of the food chain, it is important to consider how students spend the bulk of their time. In the first scenario, students are most likely engaged in finding and reporting information. Doing so will lead them to some level of understanding of the food chain, but the work is primarily "regurgitation" of content. The second scenario assumes students have already found their information and are reporting it using a digital presentation, which is a worthy goal. Their engagement, however, is now in the digital presentation software. Again, although the students are focusing on important skills, as the teacher, you must consider what content is the *goal* of instruction. In this case, students are engaged in the use of software, not understanding the food chain. The third scenario has students "grappling" with the content itself—understanding the cause-and-effect relationships that exist and using higher-order thinking to consider future situations. All three of these scenarios might occur when learning about the food chain; the key is the *amount* of time allocated to each. Engaged learners need to be grappling with curricular content in significant ways much of the time, no matter what their ages.

Student Responsibility for Learning

Student responsibility for learning is a concept that most educators embrace but few foster. Teachers are often frustrated that students don't come to class prepared, haven't done their homework, and so forth. If you take a closer look at most classrooms, students enter the room and wait for the teacher to tell them what to do; or they follow a "do now" written on the board, that the teacher created. You'll hear teachers saying phrases like, "clear your desks," "take out a pen and paper," "line up at the door," "quiet down," "speak up," and more. Teachers will call on students to speak; distribute materials; give, collect, grade, and return assignments; and tell students what their grades are. In this type of environment, the teacher takes much greater responsibility for learning than do the students.

Imagine a classroom in which students walk through the door; pick up a folder, or log onto a website that includes their current work and a schedule that they developed the prior day; read through comments from the teacher; and start working on activities they decided upon. Students determine what resources they'll need to accomplish their tasks, and they sign up for them, including *small-group mini-lessons* offered by the teacher. They use rubrics to guide their work and assess their own progress; and they tell the teacher how they're doing and what they need to be more successful. The teacher facilitates learning through a carefully structured environment that allows students to take responsibility for the classroom. Student responsibility for learning requires clearly articulated expectations and consequences, structures that students use to meet with success, and guidance and feedback from the teacher.

Academic Rigor

If students are engaged in learning and taking greater responsibility for their own learning, then increasing academic rigor is easy. The battle cry of most schools is to increase test scores, even if scores are already relatively high; but you can't force students to learn. Glasser (1998) purports that students choose to learn based on a sense of belonging, freedom, power, and fun. Sousa (2005) found that for information to move into long-term memory, it must have sense and meaning. Lecturing, drilling, and forcing memorization will not increase learning. It may bring about a small, temporary bump in test scores, but weeks later, the students will have little to show for their work, and little foundation to build upon the following year.

I met with a group of teachers representing second grade through twelfth grade to discuss rethinking instruction. During the discussion, an eleventh-grade teacher commented, "Well not only do I have to concentrate on history, but I have to teach them how to write. I don't know what your curriculum is in middle school, but our eleventh graders can't write in paragraphs!" A middle school language arts teacher quickly defended her curriculum with, "I spend a lot of time on paragraph construction because they come to me with no knowledge; but they leave my classroom with strong writing skills. Our district needs to teach paragraph writing in the elementary grades." A second-grade teacher who happened to have a stack of student stories with her pulled them out and said, "I don't know what you're talking about. My second graders write great paragraphs." We passed around the student writing samples and the upper-grade teachers were incredulous. The first teacher to speak exclaimed, "If they write this well in second grade, what happens to them when they get to high school?!"

Many students can memorize content for the moment. If you engage students' minds in grappling with content through meaningful, authentic problems, they will build knowledge and understanding for the long-term. If you increase their responsibility for learning, offering them freedom and power, they will be able to accomplish more, not remaining dependent on others to continue moving forward. You can then increase academic rigor through well-crafted assignments, questions, differentiation, collaboration, and more.

The Digital Generation

The Internet has significantly changed how people communicate, work, collaborate, engage in commerce, and think. Educators need to understand how the Web 2.0 world has affected today's students and design classrooms that better suit their learning modalities.

As early as 1998, Don Tapscott described the ten themes of the then-emerging digital (or 'net) generation. They possess a *strong independence and autonomy*, considering they can easily access and challenge information. They reveal an *emotional and intellectual openness*, based on their willingness to post their thoughts and opinions on websites. They are *inclusive*, using technology as a means through which to develop a community of diverse individuals with whom they interact. They believe in *free expression and strong views*, having unparalleled access to information and forums. They are *innovative*, continually looking for ways to improve the world around them. They are *preoccupied with maturity*, seeking to meld into groups of people who are older than they. They engage in *investigations*, willing to surf the Internet in search of the answers they seek. They thrive on *immediacy*, spurred on by the instantaneous connection offered by modern cellular phones and the Internet. They are *sensitive to corporate interest*, skeptical that media messages are designed to serve corporate needs. They are mindful of *authentication and trust*, given that, with the open-architecture of the Internet, they must continually question what they see and hear. Tapscott (2009) later reinforced this, pointing out how these characteristics have been solidified in these students' adult lives. This and future generations of students deserve formal learning environments that honor their unique characteristics.

Consider a few effects of Web 2.0 on the digital generation. In a Web 2.0 world, you:

♦ Can post opinions through blogging, share videos, upload podcasts, create personal social networking pages, and more. The result is that your students *thrive on expressing themselves in a variety of ways*.

♦ Go to websites and they welcome you, know what you're interested in, and refer to you by name. You create digital avatars that represent you online. The result is that your students *expect personalization*.

- Text whom you want, instant message (IM) whom you want, engage in online environments with whom you want, control your computer's desktop, and customize your phone. The result is that your students *demand freedom*.

- Engage in online, interactive environments with others around the world, socializing, creating, and gaming. The result is that your students *thrive on social interaction*.

- "Google" people, look up topics on *Wikipedia*, run to an online encyclopedia to learn to pronounce a word, go to the U.N. website to learn about world hunger, check the weather, and get the news. The result is that your students *demand immediate information*—what they want, when they want it.

- IM several people while you search the Web, engage in an online discussion, watch a television program on computer and text on the phone. The result is that your students *want to be everywhere at once*.

- Can grieve the loss of others through social networking pages, raise money for starving people in third-world countries, raise money to support taking a stand against genocide in other parts of the world, and organize political events. The result is that your students are *socially aware and active*.

These results speak to the need to design classrooms that are engaging, authentic, differentiated, resource-rich, collaborative, and foster greater student responsibility for learning.

Stories from the Field

Whatever your grade level or subject, you'll want to gain insights as to what learning looks like for your students before and after they enter your classroom. As you read the stories in this book, if your grade level is below the story level, consider what students would need to learn at your level as a prerequisite. If your level is above the story level, consider how the students in the story would be in your classroom. Consider how you could interact with the students and teachers in the stories that are at your grade level, but in a different subject area. Avoid glossing over those stories that are not on your level.

A fifth-grade teacher uses problem-based tasks to drive students into the curriculum through motivating, real-world problems. She has created structures that allow students to learn from her in small-group and independent settings, through written direction sheets, from one another, and through websites and software. She made a decision to spend only fifteen minutes a day in the front of the room offering the daily "lesson." Even prior to redesigning her classroom, she was a popular teacher. She presented great lessons that were very interesting to her students, merging humor with content. Still, she decided to heed the brain research and limit her amount of time in the front of the room. One day a student approached her and asked, on behalf of the class, if she would present a lesson on equivalent fractions from 11:10 to 11:25, because the students really needed more information on this topic and were all stuck. She gladly complied. As she moved into her lesson, she was happily surprised by how attentive everyone was. She presented; the students took notes; they responded to her questions and asked their own. She admits she was so excited by how engaged her students were that she failed to end at 11:25 and just kept going. Soon students started looking at the clock and fidgeting. Finally, a student said, "This was a great lesson but we only had until 11:25, and we've got to get back to our work schedules." Imagine a classroom in which students take charge and manage their own time to complete assignments by designing their own schedules. Imagine a classroom in which students take charge and ask the teacher to present lessons that will aid them in problem solving. Welcome to the *Learner-Active, Technology-Infused Classroom*.

A seventh-grade science teacher has been working on making his contact with students more meaningful and focused on grappling with content. On Friday, he had planned to take the students outside with paper airplanes to conduct some physics experiments around flight. In the past, he would stand in the front of the room giving the entire class directions on folding a paper airplane, as all of the students followed along. Realizing this is a lower-order activity, he instead videotaped his hands making the airplane as he offered verbal directions. He set up a video station and instructed students to sign up in groups of three throughout the week to assemble their airplanes. Students reported enjoying this approach. One noted, "You know, sometimes when a teacher is talking you kinda zone out. And you can't rewind them. Now we can!" Students worked on this independently while the teacher joined other students to discuss the results of their current experiments. Two pairs of students were conducting an experiment on molecular movement that generates heat. They each set up three beakers of water: one cold, one room temperature, and one hot. They then introduced a drop of food coloring in each beaker and watched to see how quickly the water throughout the entire beaker changed color, if at all. The teacher listened to one pair's description and then mused, "I wonder what would happen if you used yellow food coloring instead of blue." The students were eager to set up a second experiment and try it. He listened to the other pair's similar description and then offered, "I wonder what would happen if you used mineral oil instead of water." Again, students jumped at the opportunity to see what would happen. Imagine a classroom in which students are engaged in grappling with content, fueled by the teacher asking probing questions. Imagine a classroom in which students are working on different tasks, including some that utilize video to "clone" the teacher. Welcome to another *Learner-Active, Technology-Infused Classroom*.

When I visited a kindergarten classroom, I found students in various locations: five in a carpeted meeting area, on the floor with the teacher, engaging with math manipulatives; some at desks creating ladybugs from construction paper; some reading picture books; and some at interactive whiteboards with peers matching words to pictures. I sat down next to a student who was constructing his ladybug. The conversation went like this:

Me: Hi, what are you working on here?

Student: I'm making a ladybug.

Me: And why are you making a ladybug?

Student: Uh…the teacher is reading us a book about a ladybug.

Me: I see your classmates are working on some other things. Are you doing those, too?

Student: I wanted to do this first, then I have to go to the carpet.

Me: And how do you know when to do these things?

Student (pointing to the board): See the list? I can do them in any order.

Me: Ah, I see. I like your ladybug. I see you so far have five spots on the left side and three on the right? Do ladybugs have the same number of spots on both sides?

Student: Oh no, butterflies are symmetrical; ladybugs are not.

My conversations around the room were similar. Students had three markers with their name and numbers that they posted next to activities on the board to indicate to the teacher their activity choice. The teacher was spending quality time with students on the carpet introducing a new math concept. Students who needed help went to one another with success. Even kindergarten students can take charge of managing their time. Welcome to another *Learner-Active, Technology-Infused Classroom*.

A high school advanced placement (AP) environmental science teacher had her students exploring population pyramids to analyze the patterns of underdeveloped versus developed countries. She posed a problem to her students: Select three countries around the world that are in different stages of development, study their population growth over a period of no fewer than 50 years, generate population pyramids, and offer suggestions as to how each country might stabilize its population. A visitor to the classroom sees students working in groups, pairs, and individually on a wide variety of tasks. Students are using spreadsheets to load data that will determine the shape of the population pyramid. Advanced students are using computer programs to create simulations that engage in "what if" analysis. Some are brainstorming possibilities; others are researching countries' backgrounds. The teacher has printed *how-to sheets* for students using computer programs. She posts a list of *small-group mini-lessons* on the board, such as, "An In-Depth Look at Factors Affecting Population Growth" and "Analyzing Population Pyramids," for which students can sign up to attend. Students are eager to share their findings and insights with one another and move freely around the room doing so. When the bell rings, no one wants to leave class. Welcome to yet another *Learner-Active, Technology-Infused Classroom*.

A Philosophy and Solution

It is important to view the *Learner-Active, Technology-Infused Classroom* as a total philosophy toward teaching and learning, not as one possible method among many that you may use. One cannot be *Learner-Active* in the morning but not in the afternoon. One cannot use this method for some students and something else for others. The *Learner-Active, Technology-Infused Classroom* encompasses many structures and strategies and seeks to provide the best possible learning environment for all students, thus being differentiated in and of itself. Mastering the art of designing a *Learner-Active, Technology-Infused Classroom* requires certain paradigm shifts that will change your view of teaching and learning forever.

There is room for almost any method you may run across in the *Learner-Active, Technology-Infused Classroom*. As you read other books and articles, attend workshops and conferences, and complete coursework on various educational topics, consider how they align with this philosophy and how they can fit in. Unless you're advocating for a totally lecture-based, teacher-centered classroom, most likely you'll find that all of the popular strategies for fostering learning will fit nicely into the *Learner-Active, Technology-Infused Classroom*.

This is not a philosophy that is meant to stand alone; it is meant to be a solution to many of the challenges facing schools today. The *Learner-Active, Technology-Infused Classroom* is the perfect solution for designing Response to Intervention (RTI) classrooms. The RTI philosophy asks educators to begin with what is called "Tier I" instruction for all students, using formative assessment to gauge student progress. If some students begin to fall behind in content mastery, educators are asked to apply "Tier II" instructional methods to get them caught up and back to Tier I instruction. If students receiving Tier II instruction are still failing to master content, educators are asked to provide them with "Tier III" instruction. The *Learner-Active, Technology-Infused*

Classroom provides the perfect venue for offering Tiers I, II, and III instruction—potentially all in the same classroom. If you are attempting to embrace an RTI approach to instruction, this book will help you design an effective classroom.

Schools are looking to build twenty-first-century skills in students. Again, the *Learner-Active, Technology-Infused Classroom* is the solution to this challenge. Schools are considering how to provide virtual learning experiences for students so that they may enroll in a course that they attend via computer. The principles of the *Learner-Active, Technology-Infused Classroom* apply in this venue, as well as in the more conventional physical classroom. Schools are challenged to design effective coteaching (or inclusion) classrooms to provide instruction for all students, including special needs students, in one inclusive learning environment. The *Learner-Active, Technology-Infused Classroom* is the solution to this challenge.

Ultimately, consider how the philosophy and related structures and strategies presented in this book address the needs of your students and of the world of education today. Apply the principles as you make decisions about instruction in the classroom.

What to Expect

Designing a *Learner-Active, Technology-Infused Classroom* requires adaptive change, and adaptive change takes time and mental energy. Embarking on this instructional design journey will take you through three distinct levels in the change process. The first is "dynamic disequilibrium." This occurs when you are implementing new strategies and structures for the first time. One moment you are excited and celebratory, and in the next you find yourself disappointed and in despair. One day you're thrilled that you found this book; the next day you're ready to toss it in the trash. (But please, don't.) This is a really important time to keep a journal (written or digital) to track your experiences, successes, and challenges. The act of writing allows you to reflect on events and learn from them. A year from now, the journal will be a wonderful documentation of an amazing journey in instructional design. One fourth-grade teacher kept a journal. In her second year, she complained that her students were just not as good at the *Learner-Active, Technology-Infused Classroom* as her last year's class. Then one day she sat down and read her journal from the prior year. She realized that she spent much more time in the fall teaching them the structures. In fact, last year's students weren't all that good at this learning environment either, but she helped them understand it. This year, she just assumed she was going to have students who were starting the year as if they were last year's students at the end of the year. Keeping a journal can provide you with important insights, particularly in your first year of designing a *Learner-Active, Technology-Infused Classroom*.

This first phase of the change process typically lasts a year or less. Once you begin to repeat the instructional design process with a new set of students, you move to the next phase.

Human beings, by nature, seek stability. The early stages of the change process are often unnerving, so a natural inclination is to find those structures or strategies that appear to work the best and adopt them as the definitive solution. This causes you to enter the second phase: "contrived equilibrium." You'll design a rubric, for example, to which students respond well; and you'll decide that all rubrics should always be written in this exact, same way. This is a dangerous phase where often teachers are asked to provide turnkey training and walk others down the exact path they have taken to designing the *Learner-Active, Technology-Infused Classroom*. While you may enjoy the successful achievement of your goals, the journey is truly just beginning. This phase can last a year, a few years, or, in some cases, the length of your career. The key is to push on to the third phase through continual reflective practice.

The third, and destination, phase of the change process in designing *Learner-Active, Technology-Infused Classrooms* is that of "reflective practitioner." Arriving at this phase means you are continually questioning the structures and strategies you employ and making adjustments along the way. Times change, society changes, students change; and masterful teachers adapt their classroom practices accordingly. Returning to the earlier example, you may find that different styles of rubrics work for different students under different circumstances. You may modify your rubrics based on the time of year, the type of problem students are solving, and so forth. Each time, you question whether or not this is the best possible implementation.

I met with a teacher to review her authentic learning unit (*ALU*) and offered several suggestions for improving it. She exclaimed, "You know, *you* wrote this with me three years ago." I smiled and shouted, "I've evolved!" What was acceptable to me three years prior was no longer good enough. Reflective practitioners eagerly open their practice to their own critique and that of others.

Although you may think you can begin at phase three, the instructional design work that lies ahead takes time and is like learning any new skill. Let's face it, if you take up diving, you don't expect to enter the Olympics the following year. Only time will produce improved results. Use a journal or other means to continually reflect on strategies and structures you are trying and how they worked out. When something does not appear to work, avoid the temptation to revert to former methods. Probe more deeply to consider what structure or strategy you could change to make it work. If you reflect on the situation, you will push yourself to find the key to success.

I worked with an extremely talented first-grade teacher, schooled with innovative methods from the Bank Street College and Columbia University.

I visited her classroom one day while her students were working on math activities related to place value. She had a collection of activity boxes and regularly introduced new ones to the students during their morning meeting time. During math time, pairs of students would select a box and work on the activity. I noticed two girls opening a box and looking perplexed; neither of them could remember what to do with this particular activity. I pointed out two boys who had just completed the activity and suggested they ask them. The girls looked at the boys, then looked back at me and said, in unison, "nah" and proceeded to select another box. I thought this was very funny and shared the story with the teacher, who was, to my surprise, horrified. "I should have been there for them. I should have helped them through it." I pointed out that with twelve pairs of students working on these math tasks, it would be impossible to be present to facilitate every student at the point of needing help. Regardless of your grade level, you no doubt have encountered similar situations. I used this opportunity to introduce the idea of students scheduling their own time. Some activities are what I refer to as "teacher intensive," where students benefit from the oversight and probing questions from teachers. Engaging in a math activity through which students are just learning about place value would be "teacher intensive," as would students conducting and analyzing results from experiments, following a recipe for the first time, and applying a mathematical formula for the first time. Other activities are "non–teacher intensive," where students can work independent of the teacher with success. I asked her what types of activities her students would be engaged in during the day that did not require her to be overly attentive to them. She mentioned buddy reading and journal writing, where students typically engaged in these activities with little participation from her. I suggested that she tell the students that they had to spend a certain amount of time on each of these three activities (math boxes, buddy reading, and journal writing) but they could choose any order they wished.

At first, the teacher was skeptical her students could succeed at this, as she kept fairly tight control over the classroom activities. Over lunch, she pondered the idea and decided to try it. I walked into the classroom in the afternoon and there were her students with their schedules in which they ordered the activities, all going about their work. Sure enough, only a handful of students were working on their math boxes at any given time, allowing her to spend much more quality time with them ensuring they were building the right understanding of place value.

At one point, the teacher pointed out to me a student who seemed to be rather disoriented, walking around the room with no apparent purpose. Her response was, "See, this really doesn't work for special education students. He's supposed to be buddy reading now." It would be easy for her to have dismissed the idea of students scheduling their own time. In reality, she just needed to add a structure. I talked about how primary students, at first, do not know how to line up for, say, art class. So the teacher deliberately walks them through one step at a time: clear your desks, sit quietly, table one get on line, nice and straight, and so forth. By the next month, the teacher is usually simply saying, "line up for art class." So together, we developed a checklist for buddy reading: find a book, find a buddy, find an open spot on the floor, sit down cross-legged facing one another, and so forth (Figure 1.1). The teacher introduced the checklist to the students who needed guidance. They learned the steps to follow the checklist, and it worked! So as you reflect upon your challenges, always consider you might just need to add another structure or strategy.

Figure 1.1. Buddy-Reading Checklist

☐ Get your reading book.

☐ Find your buddy.

☐ Find a quiet, empty spot to read.

☐ Sit down knee to knee.

☐ Open your books.

☐ Decide who will read first.

☐ Read one page while the buddy follows along.

☐ Switch roles.

☐ Read for at least 10 minutes.

Imagine, Consider, Create

As you work to design your *Learner-Active, Technology-Infused Classroom*, take time to *imagine* the possibilities, *consider* the research and experience of others, and then *create* your classroom. When you reach the *create* sections, I encourage you to stop and spend some time designing the materials being described. You'll note that there will be some structures and strategies that you already use, some that you can easily envision adding to your repertoire, and some that you feel will absolutely not work in your classroom. Start by adding those that make the most sense to you; but never lose track of those seemingly impossible ideas. Keep them in your journal and return to them down the road.

2

Start with a Core Problem for Students to Solve

It's Tuesday and a fifth-grade teacher is presenting his students with a lesson on ratio and proportion. Why? Because this is where it falls in the curriculum. He's a dynamic teacher who presents the material well. He uses video and an interactive whiteboard to make his presentation more powerful. As you watch, you wonder what his students are thinking, how interested they are in ratio and proportion, and whether they see the need for this skill in their lives.

Next door, his colleague has just presented her students with an opportunity. They are to work in groups to propose a redesign for how the classroom might be arranged to better appeal to today's students and the work that lies ahead for the remainder of the school year. Given a set of parameters and goals for the instructional setting, they are to design a scale drawing of the room they envision. Excitedly, the students begin working. Some start to measure the perimeter of the room. Suddenly, you see the bigger picture. At the point at which the students need to convert their figures to a smaller scale, they will need the skills related to ratio and proportion and the teacher will have a captive audience as she presents those skills.

The first teacher relies on his charismatic personality and interesting delivery to engage his students. It's hard to tell if students are driven by the subject matter or by him. In contrast, the second teacher develops an activity that will allow students to take charge of their learning, producing a need for her students to learn the desired skills—not just a need she presents intellectually, but a need that her students *feel* because they cannot complete the task without these skills. People learn best from a *felt need*.

The first step to engaging students' minds and getting them grappling with content is to provide them with a *felt need* to learn. *Problem-based learning* provides an excellent venue for creating *felt need*. The more authentic the problem, the more likely students will be to want to tackle it, learn, and then work tirelessly toward their goal.*

CONSIDER

Learning from a Felt Need

Think about all that you have learned in school, and all that you remember. Can you name the six noble gases? Can you state the cause of the French and Indian War? Can you explain the relationship between the length of the hypotenuse and the length of the legs of a right triangle? Can you define a chromatic scale? Can you factor a polynomial? Can you identify the number of lines and rhyming scheme of an English sonnet? Can you name three artists from the Renaissance period? Most likely, you learned *all* of that in school; yet for many, it is difficult to recall the answers to all of these questions.

Can you offer directions for how to get from your house to your place of work or school? Can you tell someone how to succeed at your favorite hobby? Can you explain how to make an appointment for a haircut? Can you recite the lyrics to a favorite song? Can you explain how to brush your teeth? Chances are, these questions are slightly less challenging than the previous. Why? In the case of this set of questions, you most likely had a *felt need* at some point to learn this information; you built this knowledge in an authentic context; and you most likely use it often. You may have learned the information in the former set of questions well enough to succeed on a test, but how much of that knowledge did you retain?

As a teacher, it is sad to think that your students will never remember much of what you will teach them. That's a lot of time and energy on your part to reap little return on investment. Clearly, part of schooling is mastering the art and science of learning, so it may not be so important to remember some of the content. However, given that people learn best when they have a *felt need* to learn, teachers could improve students' retention if they positioned content to be presented within an authentic context.

---

* The phrases "project based" and "problem based" are often used interchangeably. For the purposes of this book, project-based learning could involve closed-ended problems, such as designing a model of a cell. *Problem-based learning* involves solving open-ended problems, such as determining how single-cell organisms could clean up oil spills. In this way, *problem-based learning* is a subset of project-based learning. Here, you will focus on *problem-based learning* to truly engage students in the process of grappling with content.

My first memorable experience related to learning from a *felt need* was at age twelve years, when I decided to build a tree house. I started nailing boards to trees, and my father stopped me, pointing out that I really should start with blueprints. Together we created a scale drawing of the proposed tree house. I had a *felt need* to learn ratio and proportion. We then framed out the house with studs, 16-inches on center, as they say in the building industry; we were doing this the right way! This tree house wouldn't have any ordinary ladder; we designed a staircase. I had a *felt need* to learn how to use a protractor. What an exciting project it was. I later became a math teacher.

Frank Smith (1998) distinguishes between classic learning, which develops "inconspicuously and effortlessly" from a *felt need* in our everyday lives, and official learning, which is intended to develop from hard work and a structured, controlled teaching approach. He points out that by the time they enter school, children have learned about 10,000 words without any formal education. Teachers complain the students can't learn the twenty vocabulary words on the weekly list; but the research shows that young children are learning 2,000 words a year without formal training. Perhaps one of the differentiating factors is *felt need*.

From Skills First to Application First

It's time to consider a necessary paradigm shift for your classroom (Figure 2.1). The conventional approach to instruction has been to teach lower-order skills first, and then to provide a problem through which students can apply those skills, often known as the culminating project.

Figure 2.1. Paradigm Shift

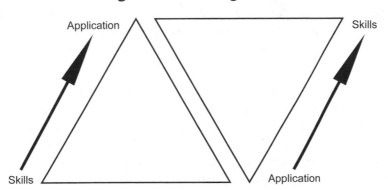

For example, the teacher presents lessons on the geography of their state; students create maps; they graph population growth around the state; they research the wetlands and the topography of the region. Near the end of the unit, the students who have completed their work are presented with a project: decide where the state should build its next airport.

While this may seem like an interesting question to pursue, the problem lies in the teacher's approach. Initial mastery is assessed in the absence of application. The dangers here are that students may not see the need for isolated skills and therefore not fully engage themselves in the learning process, and that some students may never, in the teacher's mind, excel to the point of the problem-solving phase and thus remain at the bottom of Bloom's Taxonomy indefinitely!

Instead, instruction should begin with an authentic, open-ended problem that presents a context for learning. Opening a unit of study with the Airport Problem (see Appendix A, page 148), thus placing students in the position of researcher and recommendation maker, creates "buy in," as students know this situation could actually occur. The open-endedness inspires students to create, and therefore control, the subject matter. Once students possess a *felt need* for skills, teachers can provide opportunities through which students can learn. Learning becomes meaningful and interesting. This requires shifting an age-old paradigm of the teaching–learning process: from teacher as information deliverer to teacher as learning facilitator. This shift is made easier by the advent of computer technology in classrooms. Computer technology and Internet access provide educators with exceptional resources for both setting the context and building the skills.

Let's see how this might play out in the classroom. (Some of the vocabulary here may be new to you, but all of the terms are introduced in subsequent chapters.) A teacher is about to start a unit on single-cell organisms. We all learned about paramecium and amoeba; we looked at them under microscopes; we drew them; we identified their parts and were able to see how they perform the various functions of living beings. Consider how this teacher might build a scenario to set the context for learning:

> The side effect of research and exploration of nuclear power is radioactive wastewater. In recent years, scientists have discovered single-cell organisms that convert radioactive uranium in water to solid uraninite, which can then be removed from the water. Your job is to gain an understanding of these single-cell organisms so that you can propose a viable solution to cleaning up radioactive wastewater at a particular site.

The teacher has set the stage for learning about single-cell organisms (see Appendix B, page 150). She is attempting to create a *felt need* for the subject-area content. Consider how this will play out in the classroom. First, she'll present the scenario and distribute an *analytic rubric* to the class, asking students to carefully read the Practitioner, or grade-level, column and make a list of what they're going to need to know. Then she will lead a class discussion on the task, what they will need to know, and how they're going to find the information they need. From there, she will carefully craft a *scaffold for learning* to provide varied opportunities for students to learn. This scaffold will include certain whole-class, *benchmark lessons*, such as an overview of the role of single-cell organisms on Earth or the functions of living things. It will include some *small-group mini-lessons* for those students who need help in certain concepts or skills, such as scanning reference materials, drawing to scale, the functions of various parts of a single-cell organism, and so forth. For some skills, such as creating hyperlinks in a document, a *how-to sheet* of instructions or a podcast will provide the direct instruction needed. *Peer experts*, various related assignments, quizzes, tests, websites, computer software, microscopes set up with organism samples, and more will complete the *scaffold for learning*. The teacher will ask the groups to determine how they will tackle the problem. She'll be looking for a mix between individual work and collaborative work. Individuals will be expected to conduct information searches and write summaries, draw at least one diagram, and brainstorm predictions. Group members will come together to share information, discuss predictions, and plan the final proposal.

Many of the activities that will take place in the class will be the kind of activities that take place in most good classrooms today, with three major exceptions. First, the *problem-based task* is given up front to build a *felt need* for learning. Second, the *analytic rubric* is used to guide instruction, not merely to assess a final project. Third, not all students are doing the same thing at the same time. Students plan how they will use their time, thus maximizing classroom resources and building the kinds of project-management skills needed in twenty-first century society. Designing your instructional units so that students are learning from a *felt need* will increase the probability that they will engage in learning, master content, and retain it throughout their lives.

In the *Learner-Active, Technology-Infused Classroom*, teachers design authentic, open-ended problems to create a *felt need* for students to learn the required content. This authentic learning unit (*ALU*) serves as the cornerstone of the learning experience. Given a well-crafted *ALU*, students can identify what they know and what they need to learn, make decisions about activities in which they will engage, monitor their own progress, and take responsibility for their own learning. Although learning to craft an exceptional *ALU* at first takes time and patience, the results in the classroom will make the investment worthwhile.

CREATE

Think about your classroom and the content you need to teach. Your goal is to develop an authentic, open-ended task that will create a *felt need* for your students to learn skills. Here are some guiding steps to developing your task. If you find yourself having difficulty with any of the steps, return to the previous step and rethink your decisions:

Step 1: Start with the Standards

A well-crafted *ALU* starts with curricular standards. Consider your curriculum and identify the general content, skills, and concepts you plan to teach over a three- to five-week period of time. If you are a primary-grades teacher (Kindergarten to second grade), consider a two- to three-week period. If you are an intermediate-grades teacher (third to fifth grade), consider a three- to four-week period. For middle grades, high school, and college, consider a four- to five-week period of time. Units that run for longer than five weeks tend to become too complex, and students can lose focus on important content. Units that run for fewer than two weeks tend to be too labor intensive to design and don't allow students to explore content with much depth.

As you begin the process, make a list of the concepts and skills you plan to teach over the specified period of time. It's important that your unit not exceed the amount of time you would normally allocate for the content. If your content focus is too limited—for example, reading a map scale—it may be difficult to identify an authentic problem to solve, and you will not cover enough content in the time period. If your content is too broad—such as geography—it may be difficult to identify an authentic problem to solve that covers all of the curricular skills.

You may also find that as you map out your concepts and skills, several that may have been originally slated for different times of the year will intertwine. For example, in *Ski Indoors* (see Appendix C, page 154), the focal content is graphing linear equations and calculating the slope of a line. However, in researching indoor ski domes, you are provided with the height of the slope and the distance down the slope, but not the amount of space required to contain the slope in a building from the starting to ending points. Calculating this produces a *felt need* for the Pythagorean Theorem, which is not typically taught in conjunction with linear equations, but is a perfect fit here. So be open to cross-unit content connections when generating authentic problems.

Step 2: Think Application

Suppose your students did, in fact, master all of that content. What could they do with it? What problems could they solve? Why do students need the information? If you have trouble identifying a problem task, you might be looking at too narrow a topic. Try combining topics. In the earlier example of single-cell organisms, you would be hard-pressed to come up with a task for the function of the nucleus; it's much easier to design a task around the broader topic.

Start by asking yourself, "When would someone use this knowledge?" After you respond, once again, ask yourself, "So what?" That will drive you to consider how important that application of the knowledge is. Once you defend your answer, ask, "But why?" As you continually apply the "Why?" and "So What?" questions, you will hone in on an interesting problem. Below are a few internal dialogues from those who have developed *ALUs*.

> Students need to know how the United States became a country because it's important to understand the history of our country. *Why?* Because history often repeats itself. *So what?* Well, the history of our country's emergence may repeat itself in the world today. *Why?* Well, ultimately human beings seek independence and control over their lives. Ahhhh, so perhaps students should consider a country today that the United Nations has identified as being under colonial rule and study the U.S. Revolutionary War through the lens of deciding what lessons can be applied to this other country's situation.

In this case (see Appendix D, page 158), the students would not be expected to spend an inordinate amount of time studying the other country, as that would represent too much of a departure from the curriculum. They might, however, research a country for homework to set the context for studying the American Revolution. Throughout their study, they would keep track of similarities and differences in the histories of the two countries.

> Young readers need to identify the parts of a story, such as character, setting, and plot. *Why?* Because books and the stories in them have these critical components. *So what?* It's important to consider these three and the interplay that exists in the story. *Why?* Because it offers the student a better understanding of the story and how the author constructed it. *So what?* Well, authors need to create a believable plot that depends upon characters and setting. Ahhh, so perhaps students could write a letter to a favorite author, suggesting that the author write a next book about the student's city or town, thus requiring the student to reference character, setting, and plot to make a persuasive argument.

This first- or second-grade unit (see Appendix E, page 165), although it can easily be modified for other grade levels, is an example of an *ALU* that actually covers a myriad of skills in the areas of reading, letter writing, and persuasive writing. Teachers could have students send their letters to the authors, thus adding relevancy to the task.

Given that today's Web-savvy students are aware of and interested in the real world, problems derived from reality are often very motivating. A great source of real-world problems is the news. Peruse newspapers, news shows, and the Internet, and you are likely to find a wealth of ideas from which to write your authentic problems.

Your objective is to arrive at an authentic, open-ended problem that will intrigue and motivate students and build a *felt need* to learn the content. As you brainstorm, generate as many different ideas as you can before you commit to one. It is often tempting to take the first idea that comes to mind; but the best idea generally emerges a little farther into the brainstorming process.

Step 3: Think Authenticity and Relevancy

Remember, brain research (Sousa, 2005) tells us that for information to settle into long-term memory, it must make sense and have meaning. Consider this exercise from James Adams' book, *Conceptual Blockbusting* (1990). For best results, cover the rest of the page and only uncover the text as you read it. Take a look at the list of words below for about eight seconds and try to memorize them.

> saw, when, panicked, Jim, ripped, haystack, the, relaxed, when, cloth, the, but, he

Chances are, you can remember about seven of the thirteen words: the typical number of disconnected pieces of information the human brain can remember at once. Now look at the same words below for a few seconds to see if it's easier to remember them.

> Jim panicked when the cloth ripped, but relaxed when he saw the haystack.

Most people find it easier to remember the words once they are presented in a sentence, because arranged into a sentence, *they make sense*. Can you remember the sentence? Most people still have difficulty. What if I told you that Jim was jumping out of a plane using a parachute? Look at the sentence one more time. Now the sentence is even easier to remember. The context provides *meaning*. When you present content to your students in the absence of sense and meaning, it appears like those thirteen disconnected words.

Ensuring that content is presented with sense and meaning can be accomplished by providing students with authentic contexts for learning the content. Authenticity means that a problem is realistic, could happen, or could fall into the realm of science fiction. For primary-grades students, authenticity expands to the type of fantasy that is appropriate for the grade level. After all, in the life of a primary-grade student, animals *do* talk.

Relevance means that the problem could actually occur in a student's life at that time. Thus, relevant tasks are a subset of authentic tasks. For example, when you ask a student to consider where the governor might construct a new airport, you have posed an authentic, but not relevant problem. Airports are constructed; government officials do weigh in on their location; the problem is authentic. Few, if any, fourth graders are actually going to be on a committee to the governor deciding where to construct an airport; consequently, the problem is not very relevant. Analyzing the nutritional aspect of the cafeteria food and making recommendations for additions and deletions of food items would be both authentic and relevant. Developing a plan to clean up a local river as part of a grant opportunity is both authentic and relevant. To those students who have pets, developing a plan to take responsibility for a pet is both authentic and relevant.

Fourth graders typically thrive on authentic tasks, with or without relevancy. High school students tend to prefer tasks that are both authentic and relevant. The following is a chart of inauthentic tasks along with possible revisions to make each more authentic.

Inauthentic Tasks	Possible Revision to Make It Authentic
Create a model of an ecosystem and describe the lifecycle and food-chain relations of it.	A local building contractor is planning to bulldoze all of the trees in a nearby copse. There are some local groups appealing to save the trees. Your job is to identify one type of tree indigenous to the area and design a presentation to convince the contractor to spare the trees based on the impact it will have on the local ecosystem.
Using graph paper, draw as many ways as you can think of to create a 100-square-foot area using various shapes.	Your school is considering planting a 100-square-foot flower garden in the courtyard to be a home for ducks. You have been chosen to be on the design committee. Develop a series of designs for the garden, proving mathematically that each provides exactly 100 square feet of space.

Inauthentic Tasks	Possible Revision to Make It Authentic
Write a report on the characters in Shakespeare's *Twelfth Night*.	Shakespeare is undergoing a resurgence in his popularity! Create a pilot for a television series aimed at teens and based on the plot and characters of *Twelfth Night* and design a pitch presentation to sell the idea to a local TV station.
List the causes of a particular war in history.	Consider a country or region today experiencing the same type of war and develop a plan for resolution by comparing and contrasting it with your own country's experience from history.

The task for your *ALU* must be authentic. If the problem is also relevant, then that's a bonus. It is most likely not feasible to develop a curriculum of entirely relevant problems; but some of the *ALU*s you present to students should be relevant. All should be authentic.

Step 4: Think Open-Endedness

In the world of content, there is the *known* and the *unknown*. In 1940s America, people worked largely in factories, on farms, or in service areas. Their success rested upon following specific rules and protocols. In today's knowledge society, the most successful workers solve problems, generate ideas, and create. All of the latter require being immersed in the unknown and its possibilities. School curriculum today still focuses on the *known*, with some expectation that applying that content to the *unknown* will magically follow.

An *ALU* should focus students both on the *known* and the *unknown*. It is in the realm of the *unknown* that the best, open-ended, authentic problems emerge. If students are to learn about the topography of a geographic area, they could certainly create a salt-and-flour map. Such a project exists in the realm of the known. The student researches an area and references maps in order to create a replica. It may be a fun and interesting project, but it is not open ended.

Rather, asking a student to determine where the next airport should be built is an open-ended problem that exists in the realms of both the known and unknown. Students research the area, including the location of existing airports. They must then propose a location for the next airport, and substantiate their decision. No one right answer exists, as the "right" answer is yet unknown. Open-ended problems do not have one right answer. At best, students can propose a plausible answer. In their quest for this answer, however, they grapple with content, that is, they think deeply about it, question it, and think about it through various perspectives. Open-ended problems produce a *felt need* to learn and allow students to grapple with content.

A typical assignment found in elementary classrooms today is to write a report on dinosaurs. This simply requires students to locate and report back information with no open-ended aspect related to the content, and very little to the product. A teacher might assign a project in which students will create a dinosaur exhibit for a local museum with information on the various dinosaurs that once walked the earth. While this may sound like an engaging project, it is only slightly more open-ended than the first, with the open-endedness related more to the product than the content. A more open-ended problem would be to ask students to consider that scientists may be able to clone a dinosaur from DNA and wish to create a habitat in which it can live. The students would have to learn about the dinosaur and make plans to accommodate its needs, thus providing a more open-ended challenge than the other two. To further increase the open-endedness of the task, you could ask students to research why the dinosaur may have become extinct and explore the possibility that other species may share the same fate.

Engagement in learning is less about what students are doing with their bodies and more about what students are doing with their minds. Some tend to think that if students are working in groups, talking with one another, using computers, and exploring content through hands-on situations, they are engaged. They may be engaging their bodies, but not necessarily their minds. Reciting the outcomes of the U.S. Civil War as a result of students working in groups, playing matching games, and the like might engage bodies and mouths, but not minds. Asking students to propose how life today might be different if the South won the war engages their minds. They have to think; they have to apply the *known* to determine the *unknown*.

As you brainstorm task ideas, continue to refine them to make them sufficiently open-ended. Decide how they might apply all of the *known* content to propose a solution to a problem for which the solution is yet *unknown*.

Step 5: Think Product

What will students *do* to present their solution to the problem? What will the final product look like? Avoid thinking along the lines of a project, with "glue and glitter flying." A product could be a poem, a persuasive letter, a webpage, an annotated bibliography, or a series of graphs, as well as the more project-oriented posters, skits, and multimedia presentations.

Carol Ann Tomlinson (1999) suggests that one way to differentiate instruction is through varied products. Consider offering choices based on learning styles and multiple intelligences. *Universal Design for Learning*, or *UDL* (www.cast.org), presents guidelines for ensuring that all students have access to quality instruction, thus maximizing their learning potential. One of the three tenets is to "Provide Multiple Means of Action and Expression." To what extent are you willing to allow your students to choose the product?

You must first decide what you are looking for students to demonstrate in terms of content. Then you can decide what options to offer students in terms of their delivery of that demonstration of knowledge. Students will appreciate the choice of final product. Students may even suggest viable products other than those you have in mind.

Step 6: Think Content

It is important to engage learners in grappling with targeted content that aligns with the curriculum and standards. One common pitfall of employing a more authentic, open-ended approach to learning is to allow the product and/or media to overwhelm the content. Students who are asked to create a multimedia presentation about the outcomes of the Civil War and their impact on life today may spend a significant amount of time searching the Web for pictures and sound bites; they may work hard to learn new slide transitions and interesting ways to present the information. All of these are worthy skills, but they have little to do with U.S. history. This is not to say that you should not have students make multimedia presentations; rather, that you should have them use class time engaging with critical, subject area content and develop the multimedia aspects on one particular class period or for homework.

When designing an authentic, open-ended task statement, continually assess how much of students' time will be spent focusing on the primary content of the unit. Figure 2.2 represents a graphic organizer that can be used to assess a task statement. The center bull's-eye represents the concepts and skills included in solving the authentic, open-ended task that are most closely aligned to the curricular content. Concepts and skills that are related to the field of study, perhaps covered in other units across the school year, reside in the second ring from the center. Finally, concepts and skills that have little to do with the course content, no matter how worthy they might be, reside in the outermost ring, representing peripheral content.

In *Declaring Independence* (see Appendix D, page 158), studying the causes and outcomes of the American Revolution is key content that would reside in the innermost circle. Studying another nation still under colonial rule may include related content, such as understanding government, economics of colonies, etc. Designing a multimedia presentation of the findings is peripheral.

When designing an *ALU*, strive for the bulk of the content and the bulk of the students' in-class time to be focused on targeted content, with some time spent on related content, and little or no class-time spent on peripheral content. Peripheral content may be tolerated based on other school goals. For example, if writing across the curriculum is a goal of the school, then one

Figure 2.2. Bull's-eye Graphic Organizer

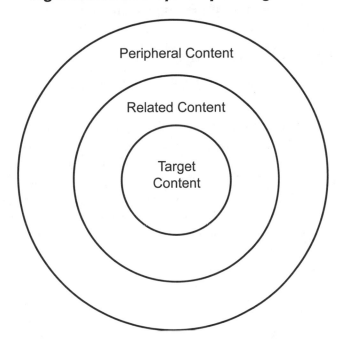

could argue that a persuasive essay presenting solutions for the nation under colonial rule is acceptable content for a social studies class. In the best case, the English teacher would become involved and oversee the development of these essays, using the social studies *ALU* as the springboard, thus allowing the social studies teacher to focus on the concept and skills of decolonization and revolutions.

Students will need to develop a product that demonstrates their mastery of the content, and, most likely, the skills involved in that product development are neither in the center nor second ring of Figure 2.2. To ensure that the product does not overwhelm the content, establish clear timelines as to when your students can work on the product. For example, have them gather up the information they plan to present and then give them one class period to develop the presentation, with any remaining work to be completed outside of class.

Another pitfall is to design an authentic, open-ended problem around a real-world event that is exciting, such as the Olympics or a presidential election, where the content isn't in the curriculum. Students are engaged and excited, but they are not grappling with the content of the course or grade level. It is often possible to creatively connect your content to a critical news event by focusing on one aspect of the event or from the perspective of the subject area.

Take a moment to reconsider and refine your task ideas to ensure that your students will focus most of their time on the target content of your curriculum standards.

A Look at a Sample Task Statement

Read through the following task statement, designed for high school students:

It's easy to take the water we drink for granted—turn on a tap and it's always there. But the water we drink every day has traveled for many miles through rivers and pipes to get to the tap for that convenient drink. In some countries, people (including children!) spend days travelling miles to and from their nearest water supply. Both here and abroad, these precious water supplies are continually threatened by pollution and development, which can make the water undrinkable and even cause our rivers and wells to dry up when rainwater no longer accumulates in these sources.

In this we see the seeds of a global problem. In towns and cities across the United States, water supplies are under threat; beyond our borders, people in developing countries have to battle against large industries to get access to drinking water. Countries on the same river are worried about those upstream polluting their water, and if there will even be any clean water left for them. There is no alternative for water, and it is essential for life. Territory, religion, and energy resources have always been at the root of large-scale wars. Could the next global conflict be over water?

Here in New Jersey, we can see the effects of using local water as a dump for industrial, agricultural, and residential waste. The Passaic River has suffered for centuries as a dumping ground for all kinds of pollutants, from raw sewage to cancer-causing dioxins. As well as being under threat from pollution, the river itself is at risk of disappearing as more and more of its basin is being built upon—reducing the amount of water that gets into the river.

At every level—individuals, communities, and governments—people can take action. American Water (the largest water utility company in New Jersey, and supplier for Paterson) is offering grants of up to $10,000 for community projects that can help to protect the future water supply of New Jersey. How can the Passaic River be cleaned and protected for the future? Some project ideas are listed below:

- Watershed Cleanup

- Reforestation Efforts

- Biodiversity Projects (habitat restoration, wildlife protection)

- Streamside Buffer Restoration Projects

- Wellhead Protection Initiatives

- Hazardous Waste Collection Efforts

- Surface or Groundwater Protection Education

Your task is to develop a proposal for American Water that will address concerns about the Passaic River and show how we can preserve our local water resources for future generations. But cleaning up one river is only part of the solution. You will then take your project plan beyond your local area and look for other areas around the world where similar problems exist. You will publish your project proposal as a plan of action for local communities in the global village.

Let's take a look at how the task designer purposefully and deliberately designed this task:

1. The task statement immediately connects the students' personal experience to the content through the statement, "turn on the tap water and it's always there." Students can relate to that experience.

2. Next, the task statement deepens the students' understanding of the situation with, "the water we drink every day has traveled many miles through rivers and pipes." Students may not have thought of that.

3. Pointing out that even children walk for days and miles to retrieve water elicits an emotional response from the students, and emotional responses increase the likelihood of learning.

4. To challenge the students to engage with the problem, the task statement presents the severity of the problem with "water supplies are continually threatened by pollution and development, which can make the water undrinkable and even cause our rivers and wells to dry up."

5. The second paragraph expands upon the students' knowledge base and presents some enduring understandings: "There is no alternative for water," "water is essential for life," "territory, reli-

gion, and energy resources have always been at the root of large-scale wars."

6. The paragraph also presents an interesting higher-order, global question to drive home the importance of the topic: "Could the next global conflict be over water?"

7. The third paragraph moves from a more global perspective to a local problem, in this case, the polluted state of a local river.

8. Next, the task presents an actual grant opportunity that exists, making the task authentic *and* relevant. (Remember, relevancy is important to high school students.)

9. The task statement then presents an authentic demonstration of knowledge: "How can the Passaic River be cleaned up and protected for the future?"

10. The bulleted list offers students choices of content focus, allowing them to specialize based on interest.

Finally, the task statement lays out the product to be developed: a proposal to clean up a local problem while making connections to other similar situations around the world.

Let's look at a task statement for early elementary students (see Appendix E, page 165, for the complete *ALU*):

> You probably have some favorite fiction books that you have read. You may even have a favorite author whose books you like. When authors write a book, they usually start with a storyboard, that is, a plan for the book. They have to consider where they want the story to take place (the setting), who will be in the story (the characters), and what will happen in the story to make it interesting to the reader (the plot). All of this is up to the imagination of the author.
>
> Suppose you wanted your favorite author to write a book set in your town? You would have to convince the author that your town is perfect for a new book. That would mean you would have to know a lot about the books your author has already written so that you could make connections and build a persuasive argument.
>
> You are going to do just that! You are going to write a letter to your favorite author to make the case for writing a book set in your town. To do that, you are first going to have to read several

of the author's books and consider the story elements in each so that you can use this information to make your case.

Let's take a look at how the task designer purposefully and deliberately designed this task:

1. The task statement immediately connects the students' personal experience to the content, acknowledging that they have read books and probably have some favorites.

2. The task statement deepens the students' understanding of the process of writing a fictional book by introducing the terms setting, characters, and plot.

3. Presenting the idea of convincing a favorite author to write a book about the student's town is intended to elicit an emotional response of excitement and anticipation.

4. Again, the description of the process of convincing the author deepens students' understanding of the content of making a persuasive argument, as this task is multifaceted, involving both reading and persuasive letter writing.

5. Writing fictional books and thus attempting to convince an author to write a book about the students' town are both authentic situations. If as the teacher, you have students actually mail the letters to the authors, you will add relevancy.

In this case, the task designer wants the students to write a letter, thus learning the parts of a letter, so there are no options regarding product. The students, however, will choose the author whose books they want to read and to whom they want to write. *Problem-based tasks* should not be written without great thought and intent.

Slow Start, Quick Finish

When designing *ALUs*, you'll most likely spend a significant amount of time designing the task statement. This might make you anxious at first. After all, if you spend too much time on the task statement, how will you finish designing the unit? The reality is that unit design is not an incremental process. Unit design is heavily frontloaded, requiring a significant amount of time to arrive at a worthy task statement. The remaining support pieces require considerably less time. The upfront investment in time and energy to develop a strong task will pay off in the end.

RECAP

At this point, you should have one task statement that you think is your best. See how it matches up to the key points covered in this chapter. Use this list to ensure that your task statement:

- Is standards based.

- Applies learning to an authentic situation.

- Asks students to provide a solution to an open-ended problem.

- Focuses primarily on the curricular content.

- Connects the content to students' lives.

- Where possible, elicits an emotional response.

- Introduces vocabulary or concepts to deepen students' understanding of the content.

- Presents a choice of product for the students to complete.

3

Designing a Rubric to Drive Instruction

A first-grade teacher meets with her students in the morning with a three-column *analytic rubric* printed in large letters on flipchart paper, the columns being "On the Way," "Got It!," and "Expert." She uses this opportunity to review the rubric for their *problem-based task* about dinosaurs. If a dinosaur could be cloned and lived today, what kind of habitat would they have to build for it? She leads a discussion on dinosaurs listed on the rubric, teaching her students to recognize the words carnivores, herbivores, and omnivores. The Expert column indicates they are to explain how they decided on their habitat choices. Today, the teacher and students are discussing what that would look like in their work.

A classroom of third-grade students are studying countries of the world, selecting one for which to create a travel brochure. They always have their rubrics out while working. When the teacher sits down with her students, she expects them to identify where they are at and what they need to do next. She then initials each box, indicating that she agrees with the progress thus far. She shares, "By the time they hand in the project, I pretty much know the grade, as I've worked with them all along to help them to achieve at the Practitioner level and beyond."

A fourth-grade student approaches his teacher to hand in work. The teacher asks, "Did you check this against the rubric?" The student responds, "Yes," to which the teacher persists, "And you're absolutely sure you're going to score in the Practitioner column?" The student looks down at the paper, smiles, and leaves, work still in hand. The teacher is working on training her students to rely on the *analytic rubric* and double-check their work before handing it in.

Middle-school students read through an *analytic rubric* at the launch of a unit. They circle everything they need to learn to accomplish the *problem-*

based task. The teacher asks the students to share what they circled, making notes on the board. Together, they plan for the lessons to come: identifying skills and concepts that are new to all and those that have already been mastered by some. He uses this data to plan out *activity lists* for his students.

A ninth-grade teacher provides students with a compelling introduction to the next unit, using video clips and news stories. He hands out an *analytic rubric* and asks the students to read down the Practitioner column and write down questions they have about what is expected of them. He then asks them to meet with their groups to discuss their questions. After several minutes, he asks if there are any remaining questions. A student asks a question and; rather than answering it himself, the teacher asks if anyone in the class can answer the question. He is teaching his students how to read an *analytic rubric* and be clear on what is expected of them.

CONSIDER

Years ago, a principal with whom I consulted shared an idea he used in a faculty meeting, and I've used it with success ever since. In conducting workshops, I'll group teachers into fours and hand them a bag of gumdrops and a box of toothpicks. The instructions are to build your dream house using only gumdrops and toothpicks within the next fifteen minutes and then be prepared to offer a two-minute presentation on your creation.

Consistently, teachers get right to work to create some amazing structures. At the end of the time period, each group of teachers shares its creation. Everyone is proud; applause is loud.

Unbeknownst to the teachers, I am carrying an *analytic rubric* that has criteria such as, "uses five different geometric shapes." Most groups' creations include squares, rectangles, and triangles; some use an additional shape. But few use five. Another criteria has to do with color-coding areas of the house; another with including interior and exterior walls. As I grade these marvelous creations, the scores are typically quite low.

I begin to hand out the scored rubric. "Team A achieved a 29%; Team B achieved a 42%; Team C achieved a 36%, and so forth." Teachers quickly reach for the rubric to see how they were scored. The anger wells up as they indicate that they were treated unfairly. Invariably someone calls out, "Well if we had the rubric ahead of time, we could have gotten an A!" A hush falls across the room and with a sigh, someone else says, "I get it." I cannot tell you how consistently this happens with groups of teachers. The teachers' own emotional response to the unfairness of judging them without first clearly articulating the expectations leads to the connection that that's what teachers do to students every day. In our consulting work, we often have teachers tell us they will never teach again without first handing out an *analytic rubric*.

In one workshop, the scores of four teams were below 50%; the fifth team received a 56%. The latter started cheering and exchanging high-fives for their success. When all quieted down, I pointed out they were cheering for an F. They stopped, admitting that they hadn't even thought of that; they were just so happy to have achieved the highest score. When you don't give students clearly articulated expectations up front, you set them up to accept and justify failure.

One of my colleagues was in a classroom decorated with Native American masks. She commented on how beautiful they were, to which a student responded, "Oh sure, I got a B. But I could've gotten an A if we had a rubric for *that* project. Who knew you'd get extra points if you laminated it?" Without clearly articulated expectations up front, students are left to read your mind; and if they repeatedly fall short of doing that, they stop trying.

The Task–Rubric Partnership

While the *problem-based task* statement is intended to be motivational, creating a *felt need* to build content mastery, the *analytic rubric* details the curricular content and provides students with clearly articulated expectations for their work. Rubrics were originally designed to allow multiple people to assess a product and arrive at the same grade, a critical reliability aspect of scoring standardized tests. Thus, holistic rubrics are often used to assess completed work.

In an authentic learning unit (*ALU*), you are going to use an *analytic rubric* to drive instruction at the start and throughout the completion of the student's work on the *problem-based task*. In this case, the *analytic rubric* offers expectations for the finished piece of work and a "roadmap" for getting there. Students will use the rubric before beginning any work, to gain a better understanding of their goals. They will use it throughout the unit to self-assess and set intermediate goals. As the teacher, you will use it to facilitate learning: to confer with the students regarding their current progress and guide them with further instruction and resources to achieve their goals.

Using Analytic Rubrics to Drive Instruction

As just mentioned, holistic rubrics were designed for large-scale assessments in which multiple raters would be grading work. The rater refers to a rubric, typically of six columns, to determine which column in its entirety best describes the work. There is a high probability that different raters will arrive at the same score. With an *analytic rubric*, each row can be assessed independent of the other rows, thus allowing the scorer to select a different column score for each row of the rubric. While holistic rubrics are often difficult for students to use as a guide for their work, *analytic rubrics* are particularly effective tools for driving instruction.

When designing an *analytic rubric*, you should be mindful of three important considerations:

1. *Performance Level Headings:* Avoid labeling the levels as grades: A, B, C, D, F. Instead, consider headings that describe developmental levels of mastery, such as Novice, Apprentice, Practitioner, and Expert. The message should be that it is okay to be a novice when you're first tackling a new concept or skill; in fact, it is to be expected. An *analytic rubric* with developmental headings encourages students to celebrate their progress and keep going.

2. *Order of Information:* Label the rows with the various components. For example, a persuasive writing rubric might have row headings of sources, persuasive techniques, facts, writing style, and mechanics. Keep those components that are most connected to the content near the top, and use the lower rows for related components, such as presentation skills. Label the columns with the performance levels (e.g., Novice, Apprentice, Practitioner, Expert) from left to right, with the highest-quality performance level being on the right. We read from left to right; therefore, increasing performance levels as one reads across the page sends a message that learning is a progressive journey. This allows students to first succeed at the Novice level, then move to the Apprentice level and so on.

3. *Rubric Language:* Given the purpose of the rubric is to guide learning, as opposed to evaluating an already completed assignment, use language that describes positive steps toward the goal. Avoid using negative criteria. Instead, use positive descriptions as to what *does* exist as opposed to what does not. If you want young students to write descriptive sentences, the first column might simply read, "writes in complete sentences." The second column might read, "writes in complete sentences using adjectives." The third might read, "writes in complete sentences using adjectives and adverbs." The student masters one developmental level and then considers what must be accomplished to master the next.

The Balance Between Quantitative and Qualitative Criteria

It is tempting to design an *analytic rubric* solely from quantitative criteria, however, it will fall far short of your academic goals for your students. Consider the *analytic rubric* in Figure 3.1 for writing a paragraph about oneself.

Figure 3.1. Quantitative Criteria

	Novice	Apprentice	Practitioner	Expert
Spelling	more than 2 errors	2 errors	1 error	no spelling errors
Grammar	more than 2 errors	2 errors	1 error	no grammatical errors
Punctuation	more than 2 errors	2 errors	1 error	no punctuation errors
Content	at least 2 criteria from expert level	3 of 5 criteria from expert level	4 of 5 criteria from expert level	includes, name, birthplace, physical description, likes, and dislikes

Using the rubric in Figure 3.1, assess the following two paragraphs:

Paragraph 1: My name is Paul James. I was born in Boston, Massachusetts in 2001. I have brown hair and brown eyes. I like playing with my dog, Mopsy. I like riding my dirt bike. I don't like vegetables.

Paragraph 2: My name is Paul James, actually, Paul James III as I was named after my grandfather and my father. I was born on a snowy night in January in Boston, Massachusetts in 2001. My mom told me that I woke her up at two o'clock in the morning and said, "I'm ready to enter the world!" Ten years later, I stand four feet tall and weigh in at seventy-five pounds and, like my parents, I have brown hair and brown eyes. Needless to say, being ten, I attend school. After school, I enjoy playing with my dog Mopsy. She is a Hungarian sheep dog, so she spends most of her time trying to herd my friends and me into groups. At night, she sleeps at the foot of my bed to protect me. I also like riding my new dirt bike through the trails behind my house. I have few dislikes, but if I had to tell you what I liked least in the world, I would have to say, "Vegetables!"

Using this rubric, both students would be considered expert writers, however, clearly, the second paragraph was written by a student who possesses a greater command of the written language. This level of writing must be described qualitatively. Consider the modification of the rubric, presented in Figure 3.2.

Figure 3.2. Qualitative Criteria

	Novice	Apprentice	Practitioner	Expert
Spelling, grammar, and punctuation	use of inventive spelling	multiple errors	eliminates all but 1 error	no errors
Content	1 to 2 of the criteria from Practitioner column	3 to 4 of the criteria from Practitioner column	includes name, birthplace, physical description, likes, and dislikes	all of Practitioner plus additional information
Sentence quality	sentences include a simple subject and simple predicate	sentences follow the same structure but include descriptive words	some variation in sentence structure, use of descriptive words	varied sentence structure throughout, use of descriptive words and phrases
Sentence flow	each sentence focuses on topic	some sentences relate to one another	use of connecting words and phrases to enhance paragraph flow	sentences follow one another with smooth transitions based on content and use of connecting words and phrases

This *analytic rubric* successfully differentiates between the two writing samples. Compare the criteria in the rubrics in Figures 3.1 and 3.2. The former contains solely quantitative criteria, whereas the latter offers descriptive criteria to capture the quality of writing beyond sheer quantity. While it is easy to become fixated on filling in the grid, be sure to read through your rubric criteria carefully to ensure that they describe the quality of the performance.

CREATE

Step 1: Identifying Grade-Level Performance

Given that the purpose of the *analytic rubric* is to offer clearly articulated expectations, begin rubric design by asking yourself what you would consider to be a strong, grade-level performance. Once you have your authentic, open-ended task and product defined, think about what that final product would look like. Write down a list of descriptive phrases, focusing more on the curricular content than on the product itself. If you allow students to choose their final product, some may create multimedia presentations while others offer oral presentations, and still others written work; but the same subject-area content should be evident in all.

If you're asking primary students to create a guide for dressing appropriately for the temperature (see Appendix F, page 169), you may want them to identify, say, six different temperatures. Temperatures should be separated from each other by ten degrees so that the guide represents a range of temperatures. You may want students to include a picture of a person dressed for each temperature. You may want them to write about how to dress at each temperature. As you think through the final product, you'll identify what you would expect. Be as specific as possible.

Step 2: Defining the Rubric Categories

Next, group the criteria into categories. In the above example, you might have "Temperatures," "Pictures of Clothing," and "Descriptions" as three of your categories. A strong *analytic rubric* generally has four to seven categories, or rows. Review your categories to ensure that they are heavily oriented toward the desired subject-area content. In the "Dressing for Temperature" example, three of the four rows reflect the content of matching appropriate dress to the temperature, and one of the rows describes the format of the guidebook.

In self-contained, elementary grades, one could argue that mixing content in one rubric is actually preferred. That is, even though a particular *prob-*

lem-based task is about science, include the writing aspects and math aspects. It is only with departmentalization that you have to take care to focus primarily on the subject-area content. Optimally, a team of teachers would design a unit that allows the student to focus on content from multiple subject areas while addressing the same task. For example, if the science teacher has students writing a persuasive argument on global warming, the language arts teacher might provide assistance on persuasive writing techniques and grade the papers from that perspective.

Step 3: Moving from Novice to Practitioner

The next step is to write an individual row or category. Your brainstormed list of expectations should form your Practitioner column. Based on each category you chose, fill the Practitioner column with a description of what you expect. Figures 3.3 and 3.4 (page 42) are examples.

Once the Practitioner column is written, consider the developmental steps students would follow to arrive at that level of performance. Where might they start? What naturally follows? Use this line of thinking to develop the Novice and Apprentice columns. Keep in mind that as you read from Novice to Apprentice to Practitioner, you want to see a natural progression of learning, the way you would instruct students. Review the Practitioner column to ensure that all of your expectations are included. If you expect it, it must be articulated in the rubric.

Step 4: Writing the Expert Column

Writing the Expert column is slightly different from writing the others, as you're looking to inspire students to achieve at levels that are higher than grade-level expectations. Essentially, there are four ways to move from the Practitioner column to the Expert column.

1. The first, and least powerful, is to make a quantitative leap, that is, have students produce more. If the Practitioner column asks for four facts, the Expert asks for more than four. If the Practitioner column asks for varied sources, including books, journals, and the Internet, the Expert column asks for two of each. Sometimes, asking for more is the appropriate approach; however, always challenge yourself to make a qualitative leap, modifying the quality rather than quantity of response.

2. The second option is to make a leap of *extended content*, that is, content that may not typically be introduced at the grade level or at all. If elementary students are asked to draw a compass rose on a map with four directions (i.e., N, S, E, and W), the Expert column might require them to include eight directions using a

Figure 3.3. Fairytale Writing Rubirc

Task	Novice	Apprentice	Practitioner	Expert
Fairytale Story Map			graphic orga- nizer shows all of the story ele- ments	
Fairytale Characters			♦ 3–4 varied characters (magical crea- tures, royalty, fairies, ani- mals, giants, etc.) ♦ a picture of each character	
Fairytale Setting			♦ takes place long ago ♦ uses descrip- tive words to explain setting	
Fairytale Plot			♦ includes ele- ment of good and evil ♦ is make be- lieve ♦ has a problem ♦ has a happy solution	
Presentation			reads story so others can hear; shows pictures to class when speaking about them	

Figure 3.4. Map Rubric

		Novice	Apprentice	Practitioner	Expert
Drawn to scale				scale is included and labeled with units of measure; scale is appropriate for size	
Landforms				includes all 10 required landforms with several included more than once	
Key/legend				all geographic attributes included in key; symbols match on map; color-coded for clarity	
Compass rose				includes 8 directions; neatly drawn	
Important places	Number			7–8 varied places included on map	
	Description			each place is described in terms of its geographic attributes and use	

protractor to accurately measure the four directions. If the Practitioner column asks students to use prepositions in their writing, the Expert column might ask them to use hyperlinks to identify phrases serving as adjectives and those serving as adverbs. If algebra students are asked to design a ski slope using line segments and by writing linear equations, the Expert column might require designing a mogul, thus introducing the concept of the parabola. If music students are asked to play a song within a single scale of notes, the Expert column might require them to play a song that covers notes in two octaves.

3. A third option is to make a leap of *higher cognitive level*, that is, requiring a more sophisticated level of thinking. If students are asked to list cause-and-effect relationships of an event, the Expert column might require them to include primary, secondary, and tertiary effects. For example, if students are to identify cause-and-effect relationships of the increase in water temperature on Caribbean coral reefs, an obvious response from some research might be the death of the microscopic plants that feed the coral reefs. A secondary effect would be the death of the coral reefs. A tertiary effect would be the loss of the fish that thrive among the coral reefs. A quaternary effect would be the devastation of the economies of the Caribbean nations. Thinking through related levels of events, including projecting future effects, requires higher cognitive skills.

4. A fourth option is to make a *metacognitive leap*, that is, asking students to reflect on their own thinking process. This usually takes the form of asking students to talk or write about how they went about solving a problem, explaining a process to others, or reflecting on their plan to manage a project. If the Practitioner column requires the students to use four persuasive techniques in an argument, the Expert column might ask them to describe how they decided when to use each technique. If the Practitioner column requires art students to utilize underpainting, the Expert column might ask them to explain how they chose the underpainting color.

A common misconception when addressing the needs of gifted learners is that because they are so capable, they should produce more. Quantitative and extended content leaps from the Practitioner column to the Expert column do not challenge gifted learners as do higher cognitive and metacognitive leaps. A well-crafted rubric will present varied ways to move from the Practitioner column to the Expert column throughout the rubric.

Figure 3.5 presents two columns from a rubric related to the study of Martin Luther King, Jr. and his accomplishments. For "Background Information," to be an Expert, students make a quantitative leap of providing more and different types of information. "Effects on Equal Rights" requires students to demonstrate a higher cognitive level by evaluating long-range effects. "Evaluation of Equal Rights Today" involves a metacognitive leap in which the student reflects on the process and experience itself. "Dream for the Future" requires a leap of extended content. As you design your rubric, be mindful of the ways in which students will move to become Experts and use these different approaches throughout.

Step 5: Fostering High Academic Standards

Review the rubric you have just designed. As previously detailed, you'll want to make the Practitioner column grade-level performance and fill the Expert column with a description of truly exemplary work. Use these two columns to foster high academic standards. If it is too easy for students to achieve at the expert level, there will be little or nothing to challenge those who are able to move beyond the norm, and average students will be satisfied with their performance rather than pushing themselves to achieve more. Be comfortable knowing that few, if any, of your students will be able to score completely in the Expert column.

Step 6: Ensuring Objectivity

It is important to write the criteria in as objective a manner as possible so that student and teacher alike will assign the same performance level. "Neat" means something different to everyone. "All lines drawn with a ruler or straightedge" means the same thing to everyone. This aspect can be a challenge; however, taking the time to define a performance allows you to raise academic standards. Read through your rubric to ensure that you have clearly defined all criteria. Where space is an issue, use a nested rubric or a checklist. For example, if you use the term "neat" in your rubric, provide a separate checklist that describes what neat looks like. If the unit content is social studies, but you are asking students to write a persuasive argument,

Figure 3.5. Civil Rights Project Rubric

		Novice	Apprentice	Practitioner	Expert
Content	Back-ground Informa-tion			descriptions of 4 key events from 1955–1968 includ-ing, but not limited to: ♦ school desegre-gation ♦ bus boycott ♦ nonviolent forms of protest ♦ voting rights	all of Practitio-ner plus photos of these events and quotes from major Civil Rights figures of the time
	Effects on Equal Rights			☐ all 4 key events followed by data showing effects in the U.S.—laws passed, legal precedents set, societal changes ☐ details key Civil Rights figures' involvement	all of Practitio-ner plus student evaluation of the long-range effects for each event
	Evalu-ation of Equal Rights Today			3 areas of Ameri-can life addressed using data and personal experi-ence from inter-views	all of Practitio-ner plus stu-dent's personal experiences and interpreta-tion of data
	Dream for the Future			☐ applies equal rights issues to a 21st century context ☐ addresses all problems identified in American life in evaluation section	all of Practitio-ner plus ad-dresses equal rights issues for other races, gender, sexual orientation, etc.

keep the rubric focused on social studies content and include a reference to a persuasive writing rubric that is a separate rubric unto itself. This is particularly helpful when offering students options for the final product. You may write a math unit task that allows students to create a multimedia presentation, three-dimensional model, or written report. Focus on the math content in the rubric and refer students to a separate *analytic rubric* for the type of final product. You can utilize those rubrics throughout the year as students design various products.

A Closer Look at Exemplary Rubrics

Let's recap some of the important features of a high-quality rubric. Consider the content rubric for "Radioactive Waste Smorgasbord" (Appendix B, page 150) shown in Figure 3.6, which is appropriate for middle-grade students. (The choice of this rubric is for illustrative purposes; you'll want to think through the points made here as they relate to your grade level and subject area.) Students are studying the possibility of bacteria being used to clean up radioactive waste. The content focus of the unit is bacteria. Read down the Practitioner column; it is full of criteria related to the study of bacteria. The first step in assessing the quality of your rubric is to read down the Practitioner column to ensure that it details the curricular content being studied.

Figure 3.6. Rubric for Radioactive Waste Smorgasbord

	Novice	**Apprentice**	**Practitioner**	**Expert**
Bacteria structure	beginning stages of diagram of bacteria cell structure	♦ diagram of bacteria cell structure ♦ images and description of how bacteria reproduce	♦ accurately labeled diagram of bacteria cell structure ♦ images and detailed description of how bacteria reproduce	all of Practitioner plus includes diagrams of 3 "uranium-eating" bacteria
Knowledge of "uranium-eating" bacteria	identifies 3 "uranium-eating" bacteria	identifies 3 "uranium-eating" bacteria and includes detailed explanation of metabolism and respiration for at least 1	identifies 3 "uranium-eating" bacteria and, for each, includes detailed explanation of metabolism and respiration	all of Practitioner plus includes differences in habitat and oxygen tolerance

	Novice	Apprentice	Practitioner	Expert
Bacteria in the human body	identifies at least 1 bacteria that is found in the human body	identifies at least 1 bacteria that has a negative effect on the human body and 1 that has a positive effect	identifies at least 3 different incidences of bacteria in the human body (representing both positive and negative effects) and explains their role	all of Practitioner plus includes comments on the effects of eliminating each of these
Bacteria in the environment	identifies at least 1 bacteria that is found in the environment	identifies at least 1 bacteria that has a negative effect on the environment and 1 that has a positive effect	identifies at least 3 different incidences of bacteria in the environment (representing both positive and negative effects) and explains their role	all of Practitioner plus includes comments on the effects of eliminating each of these
Bacteria and uranium	identifies 3 different bacteria that interact with uranium to eliminate radioactive waste	explains how the 3 different bacteria interact with uranium to eliminate radioactive waste	details how 3 different bacteria interact with uranium to eliminate radioactive waste, including a description and cause-and-effect or process diagrams	all of Practitioner plus details conditions (i.e., oxygen and radioactivity levels) before, during, and after the time the bacteria are present

Next, look at the developmental movement from Novice to Apprentice to Practitioner. In the first row, the Novice is acknowledged for beginning a diagram of the cell structure. The Apprentice has a completed diagram along with images and a description of how bacteria produce, but little is indicated about the actual quality of the work. The Practitioner column introduces a level of quality, indicating an "accurately labeled" diagram and a "detailed description" of reproduction. In this row, the rubric designer is considering what would most likely happen first, then next, and then after that to achieve the goal. Given that you'll be using the rubric to drive instruction and guide your students, keep in mind that they will read each column and decide what they have to do to achieve at that level. Essentially, you are mapping out the path to success for them. Note the developmental progression in each row.

In "The Mozart Effect" (Appendix G, page 171), students are writing a persuasive argument to convince the school principal to play Mozart's music in the halls during the passing of classes based on research on the effect of classical music on the brain. Figure 3.7 offers a section of the rubric in which students are selecting another genre of music and comparing and contrasting it to Mozart's and other classical composers' music. Note that the third column of criteria, the Practitioner column, identifies eight elements of music. The teacher, in this example, does not favor one element over the others; all are of equal importance in this case, so they are simply listed. Earlier columns then indicate a range of how many of the elements are included, but are not concerned with which ones are included. This is not the case of the next row in which the rubric author wants the student to first state a hypothesis, then look for one supporting reference, then build support with one or two more, and finally complete the same for another musical composition and compare the works to another classical composer. In this case, there is a developmental justification for the order in which the student accomplishes the criteria, so a checklist would not be appropriate.

The Grading Dilemma

The key to teaching through an authentic learning unit (*ALU*) is realizing that your role as the teacher is to ensure that *all* students achieve at the Practitioner level. Your job is to provide high-quality, varied learning experiences so that all students succeed; consequently, grading students on the final product is more like grading your own performance. The unit rubric is not intended to produce a grade as much as it is to drive instruction. If you do grade the performance, and if you succeeded in your role in the classroom, it should earn an A or a B. If the authentic, open-ended unit task is compelling, students will engage for that reason alone and not for the grade. After all, when students play after school and engage in various sports and online activities, they're not doing so for a grade.

Throughout the unit, the students will engage in a number of activities, both collaboratively and individually. You should grade individual assignments and individual contributions to the final product. Intermediate deadlines for various stages of the final product will help students manage the project more successfully, and related individual assignments should also be graded. You should additionally give quizzes and even tests across the course of the unit. All of these grades will allow you to see how the individual student is progressing with content mastery.

You will know whether or not *you* have achieved your goals as a teacher by the success rate of your students in achieving at the Practitioner column.

Figure 3.7. Partial Rubric for the Mozart Effect

	Novice	Apprentice	Practitioner	Expert
Choice: ☐ Rap ☐ Blues ☐ Jazz ☐ Rock ☐ House ☐ Baroque ☐ Other	includes 3–5 sentences each on 2–3 of the characteristics listed under Practitioner	includes 3–5 sentences each on 4–5 of the characteristics listed under Practitioner	includes 3–5 sentences on 5 of the following: ☐ meter ☐ tempo ☐ rhythm ☐ tonality ☐ intervals ☐ chords and/ or chord progression ☐ harmony ☐ key signature	includes all 8 considerations under Practitioner *and* explores how the genre is similar to and different from classical music
Explanation of Effect on Brain Function	makes hypothesis based on above characteristics	☐ makes hypothesis based on above characteristics ☐ includes reference to 1 significant event in the performance	☐ makes hypothesis based on above characteristics ☐ includes reference to 2–3 significant events in the performance	all of Practitioner for 1–2 of Mozart's works and a comparison to the other classical composer

Some teachers make the mistake of handing out the *problem-based task* and *analytic rubric* and then expecting students to achieve success on their own. Given that at the start of the *ALU* you should have offered your students no prior instruction, they would be hard-pressed to succeed. The purpose of the *problem-based task* and *analytic rubric* is to offer an instructional roadmap as to what lies ahead on the learning front for your students. As the teacher, your job is to provide students with nearly limitless opportunities to learn, such that, in the end, all of your students succeed.

Once the students have fulfilled the requirements of the Practitioner column of the rubric and have met with success, however, what assurance do you have that the students have mastered the content? After all, you provided ongoing instruction and guidance so that students *would* succeed; but what happens in the absence of that level of support?

Assessment Through the Transfer Task

Wiggins and McTighe (2005) use the term "transfer task" to describe an end-of-unit assessment. In the *Learner-Active, Technology-Infused Classroom*, the transfer task would be a focused, performance-based task that can be accomplished by an individual student in a short period of time, typically one or two class periods. The intent is to assess how well the student can transfer the knowledge learned to a new situation. The *problem-based task* introduced to launch the unit is intended to build a *felt need* to study the unit content. The students then spend two to five weeks, depending on the length of the unit, delving into subject-area content, with your guidance. At the end of the unit, they should be able to complete a transfer task in a shorter period of time, now possessing the knowledge they need to solve the problem.

The transfer task should be authentic but not necessarily open-ended. It should not require a significant amount of time. You will want to consider what resources (e.g. charts, maps, formulas), if any, to make available to your students while solving the problem. The transfer task should be assessed by a rubric. In the case of pure evaluation, you could use a holistic rubric or an *analytic rubric*. The rubric should focus heavily on curricular content more than the presentation of information. Typically, the end-of-unit transfer task asks students to simply offer a solution rather than create a multimedia presentation or other time-consuming product.

As an example, I have seen the "Airport Problem" (Appendix A, page 148), in which students decide where the next airport for their state should be constructed, used as both a *problem-based task* and as a transfer task. When used as a transfer task, the student is asked to identify the desired location and write a persuasive argument. Visuals and multimedia presentations are not required. Given that students have already studied these aspects of the state using a different *problem-based task,* it will not take them long to gather their data and develop their solution.

RECAP

The *analytic rubric* presents students with clearly articulated expectations so that they can take responsibility for their own learning; it drives instruction. Use this list to ensure that your *Analytic Rubric* includes these points:

♦ The Practitioner column accurately and completely represents the content that is the focus of the unit.

♦ The Novice and Apprentice columns offer a developmental progression toward the Practitioner column.

- The Novice column captures what a beginning performance might look like without using negative language.

- The rubric is mostly written with qualitative as opposed to quantitative criteria.

- Criteria are written to be objective, with little or no room for subjective assessments.

- The progression from Practitioner to Expert utilizes a combination of approaches (extended content, higher cognitive level, metacognitive) where possible.

4

Developing an Implementation Plan

Sixth-grade students were working on a *problem-based task* in which they had to use persuasive writing. Their teacher provided them with a whole-class lesson in which she had them try to convince her not to give a significant homework assignment over the holiday break. Using an interactive whiteboard, she posted the arguments and had the students help her organize them into categories. The lesson was intended to introduce students to persuasive techniques. Although they did not use all of the possible techniques, she was able to point out the difference between logical and emotional techniques. This was a springboard for mentioning that there were many persuasive techniques they would be learning over the course of the next several weeks. They would engage in a variety of learning opportunities in class involving both reading and analyzing persuasive arguments and writing them, while at home, they would research their topic.

CONSIDER

Beyond the Problem-Based Task and Analytic Rubric

A well-constructed *problem-based task* builds a *felt need* for students to learn; it motivates them. The *analytic rubric* provides clearly articulated expectations. The next step is to consider how students will learn the concepts, skills, and content needed to complete the task. In a conventional setting, the teacher spends much of the time presenting information to students. In the *Learner-Active, Technology-Infused Classroom*, the students spend much of the time engaging in instructional activities, thus taking charge of their own learning. Masterful teachers focus less on teaching and more on ensuring that all students learn.

One lens through which to view student engagement in learning is that of *participatory structures*: ways to participate in learning. Students may engage in whole-class lessons, small-group lessons, pair work, individual work, hands-on activities, technology activities, etc. Your *analytic rubric* defines what your students need to learn to accomplish the task at hand; you're now going to consider all the ways in which they can participate in the learning process. I refer to this as a *scaffold for learning* (Figure 4.1, page 54).

CREATE

As you work through each section of *participatory structures* below, stop and design your *scaffold for learning* by considering how each structure can support student learning.

Presenting Concepts to Your Students

One way students participate in learning is through a *benchmark lesson*. Throughout a unit, you will identify key concepts students need to learn in the order in which they need to learn them. If students are engaged in an art project that requires them to paint a still life in oils, the teacher might first present paintings from various artists, discussing the unique nature of oil painting, along with the importance of first drawing the objects to gain a familiarity with them. A few days later, the teacher might followup with a *benchmark lesson* on the power of underpainting. As the project unfolds, there are learning "benchmarks" along the way. The concepts involved are worthy of whole-class lessons.

Consider a *problem-based task* in which young students are surveying their peers to make recommendations about the school lunch program. The teacher may offer a *benchmark lesson* to the class to explore the concept of surveys and the types of questions to use. The teacher wouldn't begin the unit with the concept of displaying data, as the students have no data to present yet; that skill would come later. Introducing concepts to the class at key developmental checkpoints in the unit, or benchmarks, is accomplished through the *benchmark lesson*: a ten- to twenty-minute whole-class lesson covering a concept.

As teachers, we have a tendency to think that we must "teach" content or students will not learn it, and that teaching usually takes place in the front of the room using a blackboard, whiteboard, or interactive board. Students' brains, however, must construct knowledge. This is accomplished by having students grapple with content, often individually or in a pair or triad. The

Figure 4.1. Scaffold for Learning

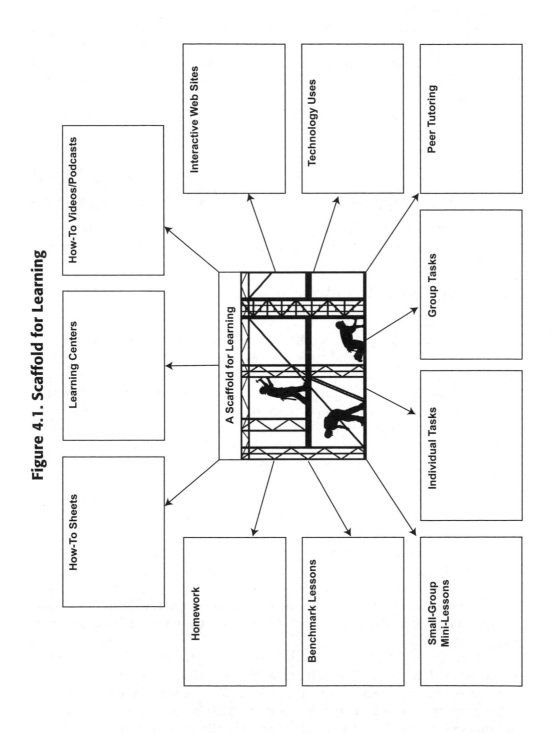

benchmark lesson is not the venue for having students learn and retain content. It is, however, a perfect venue for providing inspiration, whetting appetites, and piquing interest.

Vygotsky's Zone of Proximal Development

This may sound like a strong statement, but it is impossible to teach skills effectively from the front of the room via a whole-class lesson. The diversity of students' cognitive readiness, even in homogenously grouped classrooms, is too great. Cognitive psychologist Lev Vygotsky (1978) introduced the term, "Zone of Proximal Development" in the early twentieth century. Vygotsky claimed that everyone has a current body of knowledge. Based on your own body of knowledge, you have a proximal zone: that which you are cognitively ready to learn. Outside of that is your distal zone: that which you are not yet ready to learn. Consider a student who knows multiplication. The skill of division lies in her proximal zone because, based on her current body of knowledge, she is ready to learn that skill. Quadratic equations are in her distal zone, because she does not possess the cognitive readiness to understand them.

When you stand in the front of your class of students, and you are ready to present a skill, for some, that skill is in their proximal zone, and they will gain from your lesson. For others, that skill already lies in their current body of knowledge, and they will be bored and feel like their time is being wasted. For others who do not possess the prerequisite skills to tackle what you are about to teach, the skill lies in their distal zone. So at any point when you are teaching skills to an entire group of students, chances are you are reaching approximately a third of the class. Consequently, whole-class, *benchmark* lessons are best used to introduce concepts that relate to the unit.

Conducting the Benchmark Lesson

To maximize the brain's potential to learn, keep your *benchmark lessons* to no more than twenty minutes. As teachers, we are notorious for being able to stand in the front of the room and talk about a subject to our seemingly captive audience. It is critical to remember that while you may be enjoying your own presentation, your students most likely will not be absorbing all the content you think they are. The key is to make your lesson count!

Start with a clear, focused, and narrow objective. Avoid covering too much in one *benchmark lesson*. It's better to offer several *benchmark lessons* to build on the concept. During a lesson, the first couple of minutes involve getting the brain engaged; the next ten to twelve minutes are prime brain activity time: students are most likely to absorb what you are teaching. Then the brain begins to enter into a lull. (Sousa, 2003). Leveraging brain research, keep your lesson to about fifteen minutes; use the first few to focus your students' attention.

Your students have come to this lesson from other activities and, most likely, their minds are still focused on those, whether it was walking through the hall, finding a piece of paper, or working on an assignment. When you begin talking, your students' brains may not be focused on you. Begin with a reflection. As students are settling into their seats for the lesson, ask them to reflect on a life experience or existing knowledge they have regarding the concept you are about to teach. If you are going to introduce seasons, ask students to think about their favorite time of year and how it is different from other times of the year. If you are going to present the characteristics of polygons, ask students to write down five geometric shapes they see in the room. For elements of a musical composition, ask students to think of a favorite song. The purpose of the personal reflection is to get the students focused on the topic at hand as their brains are engaging, so that when you being to speak, they will be ready to hear.

Make your objective known; write or project it on the board. Use your lesson to create a connection between the concept, real life, and students' experiences. Where possible, utilize technology; for example, find a compelling video clip or image. Make your point, write it, restate it. Do not assume that saying something once ensures that all students will remember it.

Make sure your students are following along by using a three-finger check-in, asking students to raise one, two, or three fingers in response to a question. An exit card would allow students to answer a question on an index card and hand it in before leaving the *benchmark lesson* and returning to their work. It's a good idea, too, to then offer a related *small-group mini-lesson* (more on that *participatory structure* next) so that those who did not think they followed the lesson can receive more instruction from you.

Keep in mind that the purpose of the *benchmark lesson* is to offer well-timed introductions to concepts through short segments of whole-class instruction. Timing should coincide with students' *felt need* to accomplish the next phase of the authentic learning unit (*ALU*). Using the task you've designed, consider various points along the way at which you should introduce certain key concepts. What might you introduce at the onset? How about a few days into the unit? The second week? And so forth. Figure 4.1 (page 54) provides you with a reproducible *scaffold for learning*. Use it to write down all of the *benchmark lessons* you plan to offer.

Presenting Skills to Your Students

Introducing skills requires three essential elements:

1. Activating prior knowledge by focusing students first on the pre-requisite skills they've already mastered to succeed in mastering the skill being introduced.

2. Creating a connection to their lives and the real world to ensure that the skill being presented has meaning and makes sense (Sousa, 2005).

3. Providing a variety of ways in which students can learn the skill, including attention to learning styles and disabilities.

Right now, we'll focus on various *participatory structures* through which students will learn skills as well as concepts. Brainstorm activities for each of your *ALUs*. In the next chapter, we'll take a closer look at differentiating instruction and expand on your collection of activities.

How-To Sheets

You can provide your students with direct instruction in skill development using a printed *how-to sheet* (Figure 4.2, page 58). Students who are visual learners and enjoy independent learning may actually prefer a *how-to sheet* to listening to a teacher's lesson. Students can follow the directions at their own pace, re-read as necessary, and refer to diagrams and examples you've included.

A *how-to sheet* should focus on a particular skill, such as, reading a map key, setting up a letter format, playing the scale on a saxophone, balancing a chemical equation, etc. *How-to sheets* are also useful for teaching students how to use various technologies, such as graphing calculators, applications, interactive whiteboards, etc. The buddy-reading checklist in Chapter 1 (see Figure 1.1, page 14) is an example of a *how-to sheet* providing students with direct instruction in written form.

How-to sheets should have clearly numbered steps, with the student taking one action per step. Include screenshots, diagrams, or images to help the student understand the step. For students who have difficulty staying focused, you might add check boxes to the left of each step for them to check off as they complete the step.

A sixth-grade teacher had students engaging in a stock market simulation. Some of the stock prices students were tracking were listed as fractions. She wrote a *how-to sheet* to convert fractions to decimals so that those students who needed to review or learn this skill could refer to the sheet when needed. *How-to sheets* provide "just-in-time-learning."

Figure 4.2. How-to Sheet: Preterite or Imperfect Tense in Spanish

1. English has many different ways of talking about events happening in the past. Think of three ways to write this sentence as if it happened in the past: "John walks to school."

   i. _____

   ii. _____

   iii. _____

2. There are two simple past tenses in Spanish: Preterite and Imperfect.

3. The Preterite is used to describe actions that are completed, or took place within a definite time frame. For example:

   ♦ Juan ate breakfast yesterday.

   Juan desayunó ayer.

   ♦ Maria ran for two hours.

   Maria corrió por dos horas.

4. The Imperfect is used to describe actions that occurred habitually, or over an indefinite period of time. For example:

   ♦ Juan used to eat breakfast every day.

   Juan desayunaba cada día.

   ♦ Maria ran for two hours every week.

   Maria corría por dos horas cada semana.

5. As you can see from the examples, certain adverbs will help to indicate if you should choose the Preterite or the Imperfect. This is a list of common adverbs used for each:

Preterite		Imperfect	
ayer	yesterday	a menduo	often
esta mañana	this morning	cada día	every day
la semana pasada	last week	con frecuencia	frequently
anoche	last night	siempre	always
durante (dos siglos)	for (two centuries)	nunca	never

Podcasts, Screencasts, and Vodcasts

Computer technology can be used to create audio and video skill lessons. Podcasts traditionally consisted of audio but have expanded to include audio with images. Using relatively simple technology, you can create podcasts, recording your voice presenting information to your students. Students can listen to your podcast as needed to build a particular skill.

The key to recording a podcast is to speak slowly. Keep in mind that when the human brain hears words, it then has to process them. Sometimes, when you're recording familiar information, it's natural to speak quickly, because your brain has already processed it. When recording a podcast, be mindful of your listener's need to process information. Here is an example of a podcast script.

> Adverbs are words that describe a verb *(pause)*, adjective *(pause)*, or other adverb. *(pause)* John walked slowly. *(pause)* What word does slowly describe? *(pause)* The word slowly describes how John walked. *(pause)* Walked is the verb in the sentence, *(pause)* and slowly is an adverb that describes a verb....

Note that the pauses are at points that will allow the listener's brain to process key information that was just introduced. Use voice inflection and intonation to capture and maintain the attention of the listener. Carefully pronounce words, and avoid colloquialisms. This will enhance the listener's experience.

Podcasts, like *how-to sheets*, should be focused on a single skill or narrow set of skills so that each does not require too much time to complete. You might have a corresponding printed sheet to which students refer while listening to a podcast. In the case of the above example, you might have a sheet with a list of sentences and ask the student to read sentence number five and pick out the adverb, then through the podcast, offer the correct answer. I would not offer a transcription of the podcast, unless reading is the subject of the podcast. However, other visual aids can be beneficial. Your students who are strong auditory learners may lean towards listening to podcasts for skill development over following a printed *how-to sheet*.

Screencasts are created by capturing the action on a computer screen or interactive whiteboard and then narrating it. This can be useful for creating demonstrations of skills. Using an interactive whiteboard, you could demonstrate how to rearrange words in alphabetical order while explaining your thinking. You could explain how to solve a division problem while writing it out. You could demonstrate how to build a Punnett's Square for genetic predictions.

You'll want to plan out your lesson, again, focusing on a narrow objective. Capture the action on the computer or interactive whiteboard using one of a variety of available screen capture programs. Then add your voiceover to narrate the screencast. Screencasts, therefore, combine audio and video, appealing to both auditory and visual learners.

Vodcasts, sometimes called videocasts, combine audio and motion video. You can utilize a video camera, flip camera, or cell phone to capture the video and audio of a lesson or performance offered by you, students, or other adults.

I presented this idea to a seventh-grade science teacher years ago, before the advent of digital video cameras. I walked into his classroom one day; he was working with some students, asking probing questions about an experiment in progress. Other students were looking up information on a computer; still others were meeting in groups to discuss their findings. I heard the teacher's voice on the other side of the room. I walked over to find a group of three students watching a video of the teacher. The screen revealed just his hands folding a paper airplane as he gave verbal directions. He was taking his students outside at the end of the week to learn about the physics behind flight. I later found out that he had set up a video camera in his basement and was filming short clips of demonstrations for his students. He told me that he realized that standing in the front of the room giving an entire class directions for folding a paper airplane was a poor use of his time. By creating the video, small groups of students could work on preparing for the flight lesson while he focused on pushing other students' thinking during the current experiment. I asked the students how they liked learning this way and they unanimously agreed it was better than listening to the teacher in the front of the room. One student exclaimed, "When you zone out and miss something, you can rewind him!" College students report a similar experience. An iTunes study concluded that those listening to lectures via podcast outperformed their peers listening in person, and that the students tended to listen to the podcast over and over again (Carter, 2009).

(I recommend checking whether your school has a specific policy and perhaps a permission form for parents to complete if you decide to film their children. All schools handle this differently, but essentially, if you are videotaping someone and plan to use the video with others, you should secure permission in advance.)

Using podcasts, screencasts, and vodcasts, you can capture skill lessons and demonstrations for students to use when they need them. This style of information dissemination will appeal to your digital generation of students. Plus, you will free yourself up from repeating skills lessons in favor of using your time to engage in higher-order questioning and thinking with those students who are ready. Technology provides many opportunities to "clone" the teacher.

Small-Group Mini-Lesson

You can provide skill instruction to a small group of like-ability or like-interest students through a short lesson on a particular skill. A *small-group mini-lesson* should last approximately five to ten minutes, after which time you may want to have the students stay together to practice the skill with you checking in later. Given that the rest of your students are most likely working independently, you want to be careful not to spend too much time with a small number of students. *Small-group mini-lessons* are effective for students who benefit from in-person direction from you, and they appeal to auditory learners. There are four main reasons to conduct *small-group mini-lessons*:

♦ As a followup to a *benchmark lesson*, for those who may continue to have difficulty grasping the concept or have questions that were not answered during the lesson;

♦ To provide an introduction to a skill for those students who may be auditory learners or who like working with the teacher for skill development;

♦ To provide reinforcement for students who may need help in a skill; and

♦ To provide an advanced skill for those students who have mastered the current content.

It's important to keep in mind that *small-group mini-lessons* are not only for those students who need help; they also can be an effective way to address your high-achieving and gifted learners. In fact, a well-timed lesson can be used to motivate average students to raise their level of achievement. If you announce an upcoming advanced mini-lesson and indicate a prerequisite assignment that must be completed to gain admission to the lesson, you might find that some of your less-advanced students will step up to the challenge.

The *small-group mini-lesson* must be very tightly structured. Have a narrow focus, something you can cover in a short period of time. Let the students know the objective up front. Ask questions to activate their prior knowledge. Use visual aids and demonstrate what is appropriate. Have students repeat back to you certain steps of key points. At the end, summarize, and allow students to stay in the *small-group mini-lesson* area to practice. It's also important to be considerate of the students who are not working with you by keeping your voice to a volume that is loud enough for just those students sitting with you to hear.

Structuring Small-Group Mini-Lessons

Create an area in the room that is conducive to meeting with a small group. You might set up a table in the corner or back of the room, for example. Consider whether or not you want the table near an easel, whiteboard, or interactive whiteboard. Keep your group size to no more than six students. This should not be difficult if you adhere to the following:

♦ Structure your *small-group mini-lessons* so that they focus on very specific skills and not everyone will need you at the same time.

♦ Offer a variety of ways to learn a skill so that students have more options than just attending the lesson to learn the skill.

♦ Let go of the notion that students must hear something from you in order to learn it. Otherwise, you will be inclined to offer repeated small-group sessions when students could learn through other structures.

Given the limited number of students in the *small-group mini-lesson*, you'll need to create a signup system with only six slots for the lesson. I recommend having an overflow section so that others who may have wanted to sign up can let you know they also want to attend. That way you can schedule another mini-lesson to handle the overflow. If you encounter overflow situations regularly, make sure your students are aware of all of the options available for learning the skills. Sometimes students attend *small-group mini-lessons* because they fear they will not learn if they are not working in person with the teacher, which should not be the case in the *Learner-Active, Technology-Infused Classroom.*

Let students know the schedule for *small-group mini-lessons* in advance, so that they can plan to attend. In the *Learner-Active, Technology-Infused Classroom*, students take charge of scheduling how they will use their time. Consequently, it is important to give them responsibility for planning to attend a *small-group mini-lesson.* Avoid suddenly announcing one and asking students to attend at that moment, as it interferes with student control of their own schedules.

The best time to announce the *small-group mini-lesson* depends on the grade level of the students. For primary students, post and/or announce mini-lesson topics at the start of the morning and right after lunch. For older students in self-contained classrooms, provide the mini-lesson schedule at the start of the day or the day before. For students in departmentalized classrooms where they only attend for a class period, offer a schedule at least a day in advance, perhaps providing the schedule for the week ahead. Based on your facilitation and student requests, you may decide on the need for a *small-group mini-lesson* to be offered in the more immediate future. In that case, you can add it to the list of scheduled min-lessons.

As your students come to understand the *Learner-Active, Technology-Infused Classroom*, they will learn to self-assess and to determine whether or not they need to attend a mini-lesson. There will be times, even then, when you have to let students know that they must attend a lesson. Depending on the structures you have in place for communicating with your students, you might e-mail them or include a comment in their personal folder. I know of a third-grade teacher who sends her students invitations to *small-group mini-lessons*. What a nice way to let her students know which lessons they should attend. Providing students with tickets is another way to indicate your preference that certain students attend.

You will also want to take into account that some students may choose to attend the *small-group mini-lesson* because they are confused, but as you start, the content solidifies for them and they no longer need to participate. In this case, allow students to leave the area when they feel they have the information they need. Provide "opt-out" points at which this happens so as not to disturb the flow of your presentation. One middle school student exclaimed to his teacher, "Wow, you really must respect me that you trust me to know when I can go."

Learning Centers

Learning centers are popular in primary grades, but they can be effective opportunities for students to learn at all grades. *Learning centers* fall into three categories:

♦ Those that require limited resources, such as the sole microscope in the room, a treadmill, a soundproof studio, or a bank of computers;

♦ Those that involve a hands-on experience, such as working with clay, math manipulatives, or geo-boards; and

♦ Those that involve materials that are best kept together, such as sentence strips, map puzzle pieces, and photographs.

You can design *learning centers* for individuals, pairs, or groups. Essentially, students go to the *learning center* or retrieve a container or packet with materials to be taken to a desk, table, or other space.

When teachers rely primarily on whole-class instruction, they need a class set of materials for all activities. In the *Learner-Active, Technology-Infused Classroom*, class sets of materials are not necessary. Instead, students schedule their time to share resources, allowing the classroom to house more diverse resources. You might set up an area of the classroom with an experiment, paints, an ant farm, a model, and so forth. Alternatively, you might place a set of manipulatives or other objects in a container for students to take to their location. If the materials are flat, such as cardboard or paper pieces, you could store them in a packet or folder. Students sign up for a period of time in the *learning center* and add it to their personal schedules.

In designing a *learning center*, realize that you will not be there to offer directions. Your directions must be clear and, as in the case of *how-to sheets*, presented in such a way that each direction asks the student to take one action. Suppose you wanted elementary students to plant a seed in a cup. A direction such as, "plant the seed in the cup" leaves too much up to the imagination of the student. Instead, you might say:

1. Using the spoon in the dirt bucket, fill the cup with dirt up to the blue line, being careful not to spill the dirt.

2. Use the spoon to tap down the dirt.

3. Add more dirt and tap down until you reach the blue line.

4. Take the wooden dowel and push it straight down in the center of the dirt to the red line to make a small hole in the dirt.

5. Place your seed in the hole.

6. Using the spoon, cover the seed with dirt, packing it down to keep the seed in place.

7. Pour water into the cup to reach the top. It will soak in.

Note that each direction requires the student to take one action. This level of detail helps ensure students will meet with success and decreases the need for students to ask you for help. To help students with unknown words, read through the directions during a morning meeting. You could include a vodcast to offer an even greater explanation of the directions.

High school teachers might create *learning centers*, for example, to build writing skills, in which students retrieve a packet that includes an activity and directions. An art teacher might create a *learning center* in which students study a painting and respond to questions. A physical education teacher might create a *learning center* in which students video and view themselves practicing a particular skill in a sport. A social studies teacher might create a *learning center* in which students view a political speech and respond to questions. A chemistry teacher might create a *learning center* with molecule models for students to manipulate as they explore molecular bonding. A computer could be designated a *learning center* with a specific piece of software or Website to be used. A primary teacher might stock plastic containers with place-value rods and direction sheets through which students would explore the concept.

Keep a signup sheet next to each *learning center* with enough time for students to retrieve, use, and replace the *learning center* before another student needs it. Students will learn to sign up in advance and coordinate the use of the resource with others.

Individual vs. Group Tasks

Today's digital-generation student thrives on social interaction, both in person and through the Internet. Collaborative learning can be a powerful tool in the classroom, however, you must be purposeful in your assignment of group versus individual tasks. Students must eventually perform independently, both on standardized tests as well as in life. It is your responsibility to ensure that all students have achieved content mastery. Consequently, it is important to provide students with individual activities that allow them to build and practice skills.

The best use of collaboration is when the activity is related to *higher-order, open-ended, problem solving*. Not unlike the collaborative world of work, students should independently gain a certain amount of content mastery and then come together to collaborate. When work teams come together, each person brings some level of personal expertise.

Brainstorming ideas, analyzing problem-solutions, and generating questions are some of the types of activities in which learning is enhanced through collaboration. Consider the task presented in "Terrific Tours" (see Appendix H, page 174). Students must collaboratively design a tour of a section of the United States, such as the southwest. Each student, however, is responsible for researching one state and identifying possible tour stops based on historical, geographic, or geological significance. A student studying Texas, for example, might identify the Alamo as a possible historic stop. In Arizona, Sedona might be a possible geologic stop. When the students come together in their group, they individually present their persuasive arguments for why their stops should be included on the tour. The focus of studying states is to master broadly applicable concepts and skills, more than knowing everything there is to know about every state. Individually, students master concepts regarding the political subdivisions of states, U.S. history, geography, and geology. They master skills of map reading, reading for information, and timelines. Collaboratively, they weigh all of the possibilities, compare and contrast, persuade, evaluate, and design. Note the emphasis on higher-order skills in the collaborative experience.

Computer technology can provide powerful opportunities for collaboration through networked software and Web-based tools. Students can collaboratively build databanks in the form of wikis, building on one another's knowledge and even joining with students around the world in this effort. They can collaboratively work on documents, spreadsheets, and other products. Students are no longer limited to working with others in the classroom; email and videoconferencing can expand the student body beyond the walls of the classroom or school.

Peer Tutoring

One of the best ways to ensure retention of learning is to teach someone else, and, people learn best from those who are hierarchically similar. Children learn more readily from other children than from adults. For this reason, peer tutoring can be an effective tool for both the student performing the tutoring and the one being tutored. Make sure that the student designated as a *peer expert* is adequately equipped to teach others. Simply scoring high on a test is not an indication that the student can explain the concept or skill in an effective way. It is good practice to have the potential *peer expert* walk you through the explanation before showing others.

Once you have identified a *peer expert*, avoid having that one student spend an inordinate amount of time teaching others. Students will solidify their own learning after they've explained a concept or skill to others two or three times. Once they present more than that, they run the risk of becoming bored with the topic or not having the time to complete their other work.

Designate an area on the classroom wall or website for the *peer expert* list. As you cover key concepts and skills, post the names of students who can assist in learning them. Once students become *peer experts*, add their names while removing those of other students. This allows students to build mastery by teaching others without having them spend an inordinate amount of time on a skill or concept.

Interactive Websites and Applications

Java applets are very focused programs written in the Java computer language that typically run within a website. You can find Java applets to quiz you on your grammar skills, fill in crossword puzzles, interact with an online version of a magnetic poetry board, practice telling time, work with tangrams, practice math skills, and more. The interactive nature allows students to engage with content, make predictions, experience cause-and-effect relationships, create, and more. To locate Java applets, use your Internet search engine and type the phrase in quotes ("Java applet") followed by the subject of interest, for example, "Java applet" poetry.

"Apps" are applications that run on a cell phone or handheld device and perform a specific function. There are educational apps for students to play word games, explore laws of physics, translate words to another language, play music on a keyboard, interact with a number line, paint, see and hear animals, explore maps, and much more. If you have access to handheld-computing devices, be sure to search out and load apps related to your curriculum on them and then make those applications part of your *scaffold for learning*.

Homework

Homework should be meaningful and purposeful. There is a cognitive benefit to providing students with homework. During the class period, you introduce students to a new skill, and they spend time practicing it. Once time passes after the initial introduction and practice session, and the students are home after school, a related homework assignment will require the students to recall the classroom experience. This further solidifies the learning. For this reason, I do not recommend that students be allowed to complete homework in class. Doing so eliminates the cognitive benefit of returning to the content after the passage of time.

It is tempting in the *Learner-Active, Technology-Infused Classroom* to allow students to complete unfinished class work for homework. This, however, risks the danger of students engaging in activities at home that require greater teacher participation. In the *Learner-Active, Technology-Infused Classroom*, you are not delivering information from the front of the classroom. Rather, you are designing a variety of activities through which students will build content mastery, and you are facilitating learning by working closely with students to monitor their progress and pose probing questions to promote higher-order thinking. Clearly, some, or many, of these activities should be accomplished in class with your facilitation. If you allow students to complete activities at home, they may lose out on the richness of the experience.

Design unique activities to be completed at home, as a followup to classroom activities. This may mean providing multiple activities from which students will choose, based on their progress in classroom activities. If students are building map reading skills, some may be learning to read map keys while others are using the scale to convert the map to actual distances. The homework should be aligned with their cognitive progress. You might want to include activities throughout the unit that can serve as homework assignments. Students would then essentially assign themselves the appropriate homework based on their progress. Even the youngest students can select an appropriate assignment with your guidance.

Homework should never be assigned as busy work to fill up students' time. It should satisfy a specific purpose and be meaningful. The purpose for homework might be to:

♦ *Activate prior knowledge* just before introducing new content. Just prior to introducing students to the concept of a noun, you might assign homework asking them to bring in magazine pictures of persons, places, and things. Just prior to introducing students to the skill of balancing chemical equations, you might assign homework asking them to draw chemical elements and identify the number of valence electrons in each. Just prior to introducing students to the concepts of fractions, you might assign homework asking them to identify items in their homes that are naturally divided into relatively equal pieces, such as candy bars, pizzas, or oranges. Just prior to introducing students to the idea of past-tense verbs in a world language, you might ask them to list the verbs they would use to describe their activities from the weekend. Offer a question or task that enables students to draw upon personal experience to connect to a new concept or skill.

♦ *Grapple with new content* to create a healthy cognitive dissonance. Prior to introducing persuasive techniques, you might ask students to generate a list of sentences they would use to convince their parents to let them have some privilege. Prior to introducing ratio and proportion you might ask students to create a scaled drawing. Prior to introducing the study of jazz music, you might ask students to identify three jazz compositions and explain what makes music jazz. In grappling with new content, the student is asked to actually attempt to solve a problem or cast a theory that you will then address in class.

♦ *Reinforce content.* It is reasonable to ask students to practice that which they are learning in class. However, ensure that the reinforcement is necessary and not merely "busy work." Where possible, have one aspect of the assignment move the performance to a higher cognitive level. If students are practicing multiplication with a two-digit multiplier, include a few problems that include three-digit multipliers. Those who have mastered two-digit multipliers may be challenged to push their skills to a higher level.

♦ *Generate ideas.* Often in *problem-based tasks*, students need to generate ideas that they can then share with their peers and collaboratively evaluate. Students can be instructed to gather some information from books, articles, the Internet, or interviews and brainstorm ideas to share the next day with their groups.

♦ *Assemble final presentations.* At times, it will be more advantageous to use class time to focus on the subject-area content rather than on the final presentation. If the skills of presentation development are not part of the target curriculum, relegate the development of the presentation to homework time.

RECAP

Designing a *problem-based task* and *analytic rubric* is just the beginning of an authentic learning unit (*ALU*). Implementing the unit requires a carefully constructed plan that provides students with a variety of ways to participate in learning. While short, whole-class *benchmark lessons* can be used to introduce concepts, most of students' classroom time will be spent engaging in activities to learn and build skills and concepts. Review your *scaffold for learning* to ensure that you've included a variety of ways for your students to learn the concepts and skills they will need to succeed at the *problem-based task*. Use this list as you review to ensure that you've included:

♦ *Benchmark lessons* to present all of the unit concepts at key points in the unit.

♦ *Benchmark lessons* that focus on presenting concepts and not skills.

♦ A comprehensive list of printed *how-to sheets* to be designed to teach key skills throughout the unit.

♦ A list of podcasts, screencasts, and vodcasts to be located or designed to offer instruction in skills and concepts.

♦ *Small-group mini-lessons* for focused skill instruction, being careful not to include too much content for any one session.

♦ *Learning centers* for students to explore concepts and skills in a hands-on manner.

♦ Individual activities for building core content mastery.

♦ Group activities for planning, brainstorming, sharing, designing, and evaluating ideas.

♦ Peer tutoring opportunities for students to share their learning with and learn from one another.

♦ Apps and Java applets to build concepts and skills.

♦ Homework that is structured to activate prior knowledge, allowing students to grapple with new content, reinforcing content, and encouraging students to generate new ideas.

♦ Priming plan to promote a positive and successful outcome to students' efforts.

5

Teaching Through Differentiated Instruction

Students in an advanced placement (AP) Environmental Science class are studying population pyramids. They've gathered population data on three countries and now have to create their graphs. One student easily follows the *how-to sheet* to design hers in *Microsoft Excel*. She decides to create the optional animated population pyramids in *Stella* which will allow her to simulate the effects of various actions on the part of the countries on their populations over time. To learn how, she watches a screencast the teacher created demonstrating how to use the program. Another student is having difficulty understanding the *how-to sheet* for the *Excel* graphs, so he signs up for a *small-group mini-lesson* the teacher will be offering tomorrow. In the meantime, he moves on in his activity list to a CNN video clip on effects of population growth.

Fourth-grade students are proposing a new design for a section of the playground to be constructed at the school. They need to learn to calculate the area of various shapes. The teacher has given the class a 3×3 grid of activities for learning to calculate area. Each successive column provides more difficult experiences; the rows represent visual, auditory, and hands-on activities (Figure 5.1). The students recently completed surveys to identify their learning style strengths, and the teacher encouraged the class to pay attention to their strengths but to also challenge themselves to strengthen other modes. One student decides to follow a hands-on activity in the first column, using manipulatives to explore the concept of area. Another already knows how to calculate the area of rectangles and squares and chooses an auditory offering of a podcast to learn to calculate the area of various triangles.

A kindergarten student is exploring consonant sounds. In his folder is a worksheet from his teacher. He knows that he must complete the worksheet and then go to the *learning center* that matches the color on the bottom of the

Figure 5.1. Calculating Area

	Need Some Help	Ready for This	I Know This Already
Visual	Follow the "Filling the Figure" *how-to sheet* to explore how many area blocks fit inside various shapes. Then draw 10 polygons and calculate how many area blocks fit inside.	Follow the "What's Inside?" *how-to sheet* to learn to learn how to calculate the area of regular and irregular polygons. Then draw 10 polygons, calculate their area, showing your work.	View the "Fill It Up" PowerPoint presentation to learn how to calculate the area of 3D shapes. Then find 5 objects in the classroom and calculate the area of each.
Auditory	Listen to the "How Much Space?" podcast to explore how many area blocks fit inside various shapes. Then draw 10 polygons and calculate how many area blocks fit inside.	Watch and listen to the "Finding the Area" podcast to learn how to calculate the area of regular and irregular polygons. Then draw 10 polygons, calculate their area, and record your explanation of how you calculated each.	Attend the "Beyond Polygons" mini-lesson, to learn how to calculate the area of 3D shapes. Then find 5 objects in the classroom and calculate the area of each.
Kinesthetic/Tactile	Use "Shape Explorer," the online Java applet, to explore how many area blocks fit inside various shapes. Then construct and cutout 10 polygons to add to the *learning center* with area blocks glued onto the back.	Use the *learning center* "Calculating Area," following the direction sheet to learn how to calculate the area of regular and irregular polygons. Then construct and cut out 10 polygons to add to the *learning center* with your calculations on the back.	Use the *learning center* "Fill It Up" to explore how many cubes fit into various 3D shapes and learn how to calculate the area. Then find 5 objects in the classroom and calculate the area of each.

sheet. The teacher has chosen a listening center for him to build his auditory discrimination. In the same class, another student completed a different worksheet and is continuing to create a series of pictures with letters to indicate beginning and ending consonant sounds. Next, she will go to the recording studio *learning center* to be videotaped showing her pictures and identifying these sounds.

Differentiated instruction is a necessity in today's world of diverse learners. It may involve providing choice among options; offering activities for various learning styles or cognitive abilities; using technology as a tool for providing varied activities, designing alternatives for students with disabilities, or providing opportunities to extend learning. Differentiation is not so much what you do, but *how* you think about the learning process.

CONSIDER

Differentiation is a natural process; we all tend to gravitate toward that which suits our interest level, skill set, and learning style. A person may not know how to record a program for replay on his television, but when a special television event is going to be aired and he's not going to be home, he develops a *felt need* to learn to record programs. Armed with a *felt need*, he then moves to the way in which he knows he will learn best. It may be reading the manual, searching the Internet for directions, simply exploring the various menus, calling someone for phone support, or asking someone to come over and show him how to record.

It is contrary to human nature to ask a group of diverse individuals to all sit and listen to instruction on a concept or skill they may or may not need and in a way that may or may not address individual learning styles. Yet, this is what occurs in classrooms every day. Whole-class instruction may seem easier for the teacher and may appear to give the teacher a sense of control, but the only control in place is over physical bodies, not minds. A student can sit and pretend to be listening while thinking about something totally different from the lesson. Differentiation is a combination of providing a variety of activities through which students can engage in learning, teaching students to self-assess and make appropriate decisions about their learning, and allowing students to make choices and have some control over their learning.

More of the Research

You read about Vygotsky's Zone of Proximal Development in Chapter 4 (see page 55). A masterful teacher will teach to a student's Proximal Zone. Given that among a classroom of students, teaching each equates to a variety of lessons, this begs the need for differentiated instruction.

Mihaly Csikszentmihalyi (1990) states that people learn best when they are in a state of flow—when they are so engaged in an activity that they lose track of everything else around them. Building on Vygotsky's work, he points out that for every task in which we engage, we have an ability level that determines how successful we will be. When tasks are just above our ability level, allowing us to be challenged but also achieve success, we are more likely to experience a state of flow. That state of flow, however, is very individual. A set of activities that evokes flow in one student will not necessarily evoke flow in the next, presenting the need for differentiation.

Marc Prensky (2006) draws a parallel between Csikszentmihalyi's work and video gaming. Teachers may report that students cannot maintain their attention throughout a lesson. When considering the hours that students engage with a video or computer game, one cannot assume today's students have a minimal attention span. Prensky concludes that video and computer games are successful, in part, because they use a "leveling up" approach to skill building. When the student starts playing the game, she is at a particular level. She may have to replay the level repeatedly until she masters it, at which point she advances one level. Video game designers have a vested interest in maintaining the attention of their players. If the game were too difficult, their players would abandon it with frustration. If it were too easy, their players would become bored and opt to play something else. Leveling up ensures that as the players meet with success at each level, they are compelled to attain the next. Leveling up, however, is different for each person, based on individual skill level. Teachers need to apply the leveling up concept to their classrooms, which again, presents an argument for differentiation.

Over the years, most of the regular education teachers I've interviewed have reported some level of frustration in not being able to meet the needs of all of their students. When I ask if they only had one student, could they ensure success, they respond affirmatively. When I suggest that if they had two students, they could ensure success, they also agree. As I continue to add to the number, somewhere around four or five seems to be the cutoff for feeling successful in ensuring that all students achieve. If as a teacher you feel strongly that you could succeed with one student, what you really need, to differentiate instruction, are "teacher-cloning tools."

Much of the emphasis on differentiation is at the lesson level: take a concept or skill and develop multiple lessons so that students of different abilities and learning styles can achieve success. While this sounds effective in principle, it would require an inordinate amount of time to design multiple activities for each lesson you are going to teach.

In the *Learner-Active, Technology-Infused Classroom*, teachers focus on unit-level differentiation, utilizing *problem-based learning*; and classroom-level differentiation, relying on a variety of structures and strategies to build *student responsibility for learning*. The latter shifts the locus of overt control from the teacher to the student. The teacher still creates the guidelines and boundaries, but the student has more control in the moment-to-moment decisions.

CREATE

If you're reading this book in sequence and creating as you read, you've already considered your curriculum over a three- to five-week period of time; developed an open-ended, authentic, *problem-based task* for students to solve (Chapter 2); and written the *analytic rubric* offering students clearly articulated expectations (Chapter 3). Next, you considered the various *participatory structures* and designed your *scaffold for learning* (Chapter 4).

Unit-Level Differentiation

In this chapter, you'll design a set of differentiated activities for the problem-based authentic learning unit (*ALU*) you're designing. The key tool to begin the brainstorming process is the *Scaffold for Learning* you created in Chapter 4 that considers all of the ways in which students can learn the concepts and skills covered in the unit. It's time to get even more specific with the activities. The best way to do this is with a *learning map*, which is essentially a roadmap to learning.

Start with a piece of blank paper or digital canvas. Visualize your students tackling the *problem-based task* that's at the core of your unit. Write down what your students might "do" first. Be very specific. For example, in the airport problem, students might first locate existing airports on a map; but that's not specific enough. Break it down to smaller steps (Figure 5.2).

To locate the airports, the students might use the Internet and search for airports. In Montana, for example, a search of *Wikipedia*, will yield airports in Billings, Bozeman, Butte, Great Falls, and more. Next, using a map with a city index, students will locate the city using the letter/number designation, for example, C5. You might want them to calculate distances between airports, which would require them to measure distance and convert to miles using the scale.

You will not end up building a *learning map* for every unit, but in the beginning, it's a great way to truly visualize the path your students may take. Even though different students will approach the problem from different angles, begin with one path that you can imagine.

Figure 5.2. Learning Map: Level 1

Search Internet for Airports

Use Map Coordinates to Locate a Town

Use Map Scale to Calculate Distance Between Airports

Next, at each step, decide what concepts or skills students will need and how they might learn them (Figure 5.3, page 76). Although it may be tempting to "teach" every concept and skill either from the front of the room or in small group sessions, think about how you can "clone" yourself and provide direct instruction in other ways. A carefully designed *how-to sheet* offers written directions the student can follow. A screencast is great for capturing steps you would take on a computer, such as the Internet search. The learner can watch the screen animation and hear your narration while you're explaining how to accomplish the task. They might then follow the printed *how-to sheet* and try it for themselves. Some skills are going to be too difficult for some students to tackle independently. Measuring the distance between two points on the map, reading the map scale, and calculating the actual distance could be difficult for all students to accomplish given only printed directions. You might film a vodcast using a digital camera and walk students through the steps; however, you also might want to schedule a *small-group mini-lesson* for students who are going to require more personalized assistance.

At first, it may seem like a lot of work to map out a unit like this and design all of these activities. However, when you are in your classroom and your students are making decisions, following activity lists, engaging in learning without your constant prodding, and participating in rich conversation

Figure 5.3. Learning Map: Level 2

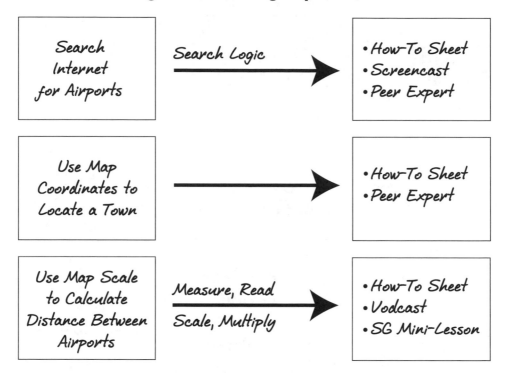

with you about content, it will be more than worth the upfront planning. The good news is that next year, assuming you teach the same content, you'll only have to make slight modifications to your *ALU*. To make the process a bit easier, consider working on a unit with a colleague on the same grade level, whether in your school or across the world.

Lesson-Level Differentiation

As you consider the *learning map* you've just created, identify a skill that is a key part of the curriculum for this unit. In an art class, for example, such a skill might be one-point perspective drawings (Figure 5.4). It's probably easy to visualize yourself teaching students the skill you selected; but for the moment, let's assume you must create a set of instructional activities for the student to accomplish independent of you to build the skill. Although concepts are often appropriately introduced to the whole class through a *benchmark lesson,* with questions, answers, and discussion, skills are best addressed on a more individual basis when students can personally grapple with the content based on activities that match their cognitive levels and learning styles.

Figure 5.4. One-Point Perspective Drawing

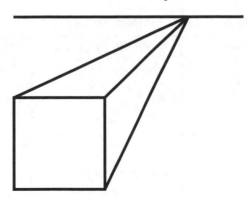

Let's assume that some students are ready to learn the skill, in this case, one-point perspective drawing. According to Vygotsky, that skill would be in their proximal zone. Consider that some of your students may learn best through visual means, others through auditory cues, and still others through a more tactile approach. Figure 5.5 (page 78) offers three different ways to learn the same skill, based on the designated learning styles. A *how-to sheet* allows you to turn your skill lesson into step-by-step directions for students to access again and again as needed. It's easy to record an enhanced podcast that includes audio and still images. Keep a list of podcasts that would help your students; then sit down and record all of them. You will have created those "teacher-cloning tools" to which I referred earlier in the chapter. Designing kinesthetic and tactile activities can be more challenging and require additional resources, but be creative, ask colleagues, and search the Internet for ideas.

What about the students who are not yet ready to learn the skill you've identified? In this case, if a student is not familiar with perspective drawing, spending some time understanding the concept will make the subsequent skill development easier. Figure 5.6 (page 79) offers the same grid with the left column filled in for those students who require some prerequisite work before tackling the skill of one-perspective drawing. Vodcasts can be videotaped lessons you've offered in the past or videotaped segments you filmed purposely to explain a concept or skill. Small flip video cameras and phones can be used to focus on a desktop or paper so you can demonstrate a skill while narrating. A geoboard with pegs and elastic bands can be used to allow a student to explore perspective drawing. In this case, the teacher has located a virtual geoboard on computer.

Figure 5.5. Differentiation Grid for Proximal Zone

Skill: One-Point Perspective Drawing

	Distal Zone	Proximal Zone	Current Knowledge
	A student who will be challenged to learn this skill/concept or lacks the prerequisite skills needed	A student who is ready to learn this or is on grade level	A student who is ready to move beyond this or is above grade level
Visual		Follow a printed *how-to sheet* with diagrams to construct a one-point perspective drawing.	
Auditory		Listen to audio directions on a podcast to construct a one-point perspective drawing.	
Kinesthetic/Tactile		Use a virtual geoboard on computer to construct a one-point perspective drawing.	

Readiness categories taken from Lev Vygotsky's work on the Zone of Proximal Development.

Figure 5.6. Differentiation Grid for Proximal and Distal Zones

Skill: One-Point Perspective Drawing

	Distal Zone	Proximal Zone	Current Knowledge
	A student who will be challenged to learn this skill/concept or lacks the prerequisite skills needed	A student who is ready to learn this or is on grade level	A student who is ready to move beyond this or is above grade level
Visual	View various drawings, both simple and complex (such as da Vinci's *Study for Adoration of the Magi*). Follow written directions to identify the horizon line, vanishing point, and lines drawn to the vanishing point to create the perspective.	Follow a printed *how-to sheet* with diagrams to construct a one-point perspective drawing.	
Auditory	Watch and listen to a vodcast explaining the elements of perspective drawing using various drawings, both simple and complex (such as da Vinci's *Study for Adoration of the Magi*).	Listen to audio directions on a podcast to construct a one-point perspective drawing.	
Kinesthetic/Tactile	Follow a podcast and use the index finger to trace the figures in the foreground and the perspective lines that are draw to the vanishing point on the horizon.	Use a virtual geoboard on computer to construct a one-point perspective drawing.	

Readiness categories taken from Lev Vygotsky's work on the Zone of Proximal Development.

What about the students who have already mastered this skill? It may have been introduced to them in another class or by older siblings; or maybe they discovered it themselves while pursuing other interests. Although it may make the teacher feel better to think that additional practice is always useful, the reality is that asking students to sit through lessons or activities to learn that which they already know will most likely lead to boredom, frustration, and daydreaming. Fundamentally, it's disrespectful toward students. Instead, consider what they could do next. You may or may not wish to allow them to move ahead with curricular content; you could have them apply the learning to another situation, deepen their knowledge of the nuances of the skill, pursue some specific area of personal interest, or even design materials to present the learning to others in a creative way. Figure 5.7 offers the complete grid, now with the right column filled in that provides activities for the students who have already mastered the skill. In this case, the students will move on to explore two-point perspective drawing. You've just explored a *learning styles and readiness grid*, a key tool for lesson-level differentiated instruction (see Appendix I, page 184).

The purpose of designing this *learning styles and readiness grid*, like the *learning map*, is to build your skills in designing truly differentiated activities. You've brainstormed nine activities that address a curricular skill. It would be extremely time-consuming to attempt to develop a grid for each skill or concept you teach. As you begin designing your *Learner-Active, Technology-Infused Classroom*, develop grids for key skills. Over time, you'll brainstorm a variety of activities naturally to address the needs of your students.

Classroom-Level Differentiation

Notice that in the case of lesson-level differentiation, students are all working on the same concept or skill, but through varied activities. Unit-level differentiation enables students to be working on different concepts and skills, but all around the same problem-based task. Classroom-level differentiation broadens the possibilities for differentiation from beyond any single problem-based task to allowing students to work on different tasks and, in the case of self-contained classrooms, to work on different subject-area content than their peers at any given time. It is not unusual in an elementary classroom to see one student working on a mathematics problem while another is conducting a science experiment.

The *Learner-Active, Technology-Infused Classroom* is the embodiment of classroom-level differentiation. The teacher designs units and instructional activities and experiences. Then, the various structures that support student responsibility for learning, which are explored in Chapter 6, provide the venue for students to make choices within a structured environment. Key to conducting a fully differentiated classroom is the teacher's ability to give over

Figure 5.7. Completed Differentiation Grid

Skill: One-Point Perspective Drawing

	Distal Zone A student who will be challenged to learn this skill/concept or lacks the prerequisite skills needed	Proximal Zone A student who is ready to learn this or is on grade level	Current Knowledge A student who is ready to move beyond this or is above grade level
Visual	View various drawings, both simple and complex (such as da Vinci's *Study for Adoration of the Magi*). Follow written directions to identify the horizon line, vanishing point, and lines drawn to the vanishing point to create the perspective.	Follow a printed *how-to sheet* with diagrams to construct a one-point perspective drawing.	Follow a printed *how-to sheet* and/or screencast to construct a two-point perspective drawing.
Auditory	Watch and listen to a vodcast explaining the elements of perspective drawing using various drawings, both simple and complex (such as da Vinci's *Study for Adoration of the Magi*).	Listen to audio directions on a podcast to construct a one-point perspective drawing.	Listen to audio directions on a podcast to construct a two-point perspective drawing.
Kinesthetic/Tactile	Follow a podcast and use the index finger to trace the figures in the foreground and the perspective lines that are draw to the vanishing point on the horizon.	Use a virtual geoboard on computer to construct a one-point perspective drawing.	Listen to audio directions on a podcast and trace the lines of a two-point perspective drawing; then add more objects.

Readiness categories taken from Lev Vygotsky's work on the Zone of Proximal Development.

control to the students in a structured environment. Students will not always know the correct choices to make for their own learning; teachers need to provide tools so that students can better understand the choices that will be most beneficial to them.

I was working with three fifth-grade teachers who wanted to run a large, combined *Learner-Active, Technology-Infused Classroom*, which I fondly refer to as "the Big Room." During one of my visits, I noticed that the social studies teacher had a group of twenty students with her in one area of the large room and was offering a whole-class lesson. When the lesson concluded, the students started working on the social studies project. Soon after this, I saw the science teacher present a lesson to a group of about twenty students after which time the students started working independently on science. After school, I questioned the teachers and pointed out that their approach was not much different from a conventional classroom: the teacher presents the lesson and then students work independently on that content. They explained that their district had strict guidelines for how many minutes per week had to be allocated to the study of each subject, and that if the students scheduled their own time, they would not necessarily meet those standards. At this moment, I will pause and offer you my favorite insight to the *Learner-Active, Technology-Infused Classroom*: If something is not working, you are most likely missing a structure or strategy. It's easy to say, "these students can't do this," but that's rarely the case.

I suggested that the teachers make the expectation of how many minutes to spend per subject clear to the students. They decided to break time into twenty-minute segments and create a horizontal bar of blocks to represent the amount of time to spend studying each subject area. At the beginning of the week, the teachers gave the students the *activity list* with assignments for all of the *ALUs* across the subject areas. As students reviewed the list and planned their days, they highlighted different subject areas using different colors. As they scheduled a block of time, they filled in the appropriate number of blocks. In this way, the students took control of how they spent their time, but with the understanding that they must spend a designated number of minutes on each subject area. The new structure worked like a charm.

As you design your *Learner-Active, Technology-Infused Classroom*, continually challenge yourself to create "cloning tools" such that you are not always directly providing direction, instructions, and lessons. Rather, provide instruction through written, auditory, visual, and symbolic means that allow students to take charge of how they will learn.

Technology as a Power Partner for Differentiating Instruction

Computer technology has the unique characteristic of being able to address every learning style and intelligence. Consider Howard Gardner's (2006) multiple intelligences, the first seven of which were originally defined in the 1980s:

♦ *Musical Intelligence*—Using computerized synthesizers, students can create their own music, record and mix multiple tracks, and analyze recorded music.

♦ *Bodily Kinesthetic Intelligence*—As of the writing of this book, both *Wii* and the *Xbox* allowed you to bring significant bodily kinesthetic experiences into the classroom that would otherwise be impossible to provide.

♦ *Logical-Mathematical Intelligence*—Logic puzzles and Java applets to explore mathematics abound on the Internet.

♦ *Linguistic Intelligence*—Needless to say, word processors and the ability to record voice appeal to those students with linguistic intelligence.

♦ *Spatial Intelligence*—Interactive whiteboards and computer-based object manipulation appeal to students with spatial intelligence.

♦ *Interpersonal Intelligence*—Videoconferencing, blogs, and related computer-based interactions with others allow students to exercise their interpersonal intelligence.

♦ *Intrapersonal Intelligence*—Building a sense of self can be accomplished through journal writing, gathering and captioning photos, and recording introspective moments in students' lives.

♦ *Naturalist Intelligence*—The Internet allows students to access real-time data from excursions around the world, such as sea voyages, the Iditarod, and safaris.

♦ *Existential Intelligence*—Students who ponder life's biggest questions of existence have access to a wealth of information and people from various religious and spiritual circles on the Internet.

Computer technology can be used to address each of these. Technology also provides opportunities to learn regardless of cognitive level. It may be difficult to provide three or four different levels of instruction for a skill without computers; with computers it would be possible.

RECAP

Whole-class instruction in which all students are taught the same skill, concept, or content at the same time addresses the teacher's need for ease of delivery of instruction. Differentiated instruction addresses the students' needs for learning. Instruction should be differentiated based on cognitive levels, physical abilities, learning styles, and multiple intelligences. Research on learning solidifies the need to provide instructional differentiation. As you design your *ALU*:

♦ Use problem-based tasks to provide a venue for differentiation instruction using, for example, the Scaffold for Learning.

♦ For key skill and concept instruction, design a *learning styles and readiness grid*.

♦ Map the ten principles to specific strategies and structures you can use to provide classroom-level differentiation, for example, by having students schedule their own time in the classroom.

♦ Consider how computer technology can be used to differentiate instruction.

6

Engaging Students in the Learning Process

A group of third-grade students are scheduling their day. One student suggests they get together to conduct the science experiment at 2:00. Another shares that he has a speech lesson at 2:10 and will be back by 2:40. The group members agree to schedule the experiment for 2:40. Individually, they schedule how they are going to use time across the day, including attending *benchmark* and *small-group mini-lessons*, pairs work, group work, and individual work.

On the first day of a new authentic learning unit (*ALU*), fourth-grade students read their *problem-based task* and *analytic rubric* and make the list of what they will need to learn to complete the task. The teacher distributes a unit calendar with intermediate due dates, as well as quiz and test dates. Students use the calendar and *activity list* to schedule each week on Monday morning.

A class of high school English students are reading J.D. Salinger's *A Catcher in the Rye*, as well as self-selected Salinger short stories, and working on putting together a letter to Salinger's estate with their ideas as to how his unpublished writings should be handled. They are also responsible for a series of other tasks, including SAT preparation work and peer editing. Upon arriving in class, students retrieve individual *student work folders*. Based on a preassessment that she completed yesterday, one student knows that she needs to attend the *small-group mini-lesson* on integrating quoted material into her letter. She includes that on her schedule for how she will spend her time in the eighty-minute block. She notes, too, that there is a draft letter due at the end of the class period and realizes that she has not yet had her draft peer edited. She goes to the *peer edit scheduling board* to find a partner who also needs to peer edit today and signs up to work with a peer for the twenty minutes that the task will take. She also has a question about one of the notes her teacher left in her *student work folder*, so she adds her name to the *help board*. Another student has already read several of the Salinger short stories on his own has scheduled time to create a podcast of his reviews of them so that his fellow students can use them in making decisions about which texts to select and read. He has never created his own podcast before, so he picks up a *how-to sheet* from the *resource table*. He also plans to spend a few minutes using the class's self-designed "excellent writing checklist" to review the quality of his written reviews before he records them.

CONSIDER

Most schools have "lifelong learning" in their mission statement; yet few engage students in learning environments that actually create lifelong learners. A lifelong learner must break down goals into attainable steps, be resourceful, self-assess, manage time, manage a project, generate ideas, reflect, and more. Yet in most classrooms, despite a great emphasis on hands-on, cooperative learning over the past decades, teachers still overtly control much of the activity of students, telling them what to do and when to do it; telling them when to speak and when to be quiet; telling them what resources to use. Creating lifelong learners means allowing students take charge of their own learning process and teaching them how to accomplish that.

William Glasser (1998) first wrote a book entitled *Control Theory*, and in a later edit renamed it *Choice Theory*, but his message was the same: you cannot control students' learning; students must choose to learn. Glasser presents his theory that, after survival needs are met, students choose to learn based on a sense of belonging, freedom, power, and fun (engagement.)

Students will not necessarily come to school with the skills required to take responsibility for learning. Teachers need to move beyond content instruction to include instruction in these skills. That doesn't mean ignoring content instruction! It means taking advantage of opportunities to also teach the skills needed to build *student responsibility for learning*.

If you were to use a stopwatch and clock the amount of time you spend giving directions and waiting for your students to follow them and be ready for the next direction, you'd most likely be amazed. How much time do you spend on administrative tasks, transitioning students from one activity to another, addressing behavioral issues? If you could regain that time, you'd have more time for students to spend on content instruction. The time invested at the beginning of the year to teach students the structures and strategies to take responsibility for their own learning will prove to be well worth it as the year progresses.

The following metaphor presents a key paradigm shift for the *Learner-Active, Technology-Infused Classroom:* moving the teacher from being disseminator of information to the architect of a powerful learning environment that gives students responsibility for learning.

Teacher as Ferry or Teacher as Bridge?*

Did you ever stop to consider the differences between taking a ferry or traveling a bridge to cross a river? Taking a ferry leaves the traveler in the hands of the boat operator and releases the traveler from all responsibility. The ferry operator tells you where to park your car, decides when the boat will leave and how fast it will move, and takes all of the travelers across at the same time and speed. Taking a bridge puts the traveler in control and in the seat of responsibility. Different drivers use different lanes and drive at different speeds. All who cross the start of the bridge at one time do not necessarily end up on the other side at the same time. The outcome is largely in the hands of the driver. But think about the magic of a bridge: a mass of steel suspended over a large expanse, being held in place almost miraculously, through the laws of physics. And yet probably few travelers hold that bridge in awe as they use it to move from one land mass to another, taking control of their travel, taking the bridge for granted.

As a teacher, are you a ferry or a bridge? Do you carry your students through the day, telling them when to do what tasks and how to do them? Do you present lessons to your entire class, deciding on a pace that seems appropriate? Or do you create the structures for your students to take responsibility for their own learning? Do you create structures that allow all of your students to achieve based on their differences? We call this creating a *scaffold for learning*.

IDE consultants work with teachers who wish to design a *scaffold for learning* for their classrooms. These teachers design *problem-based tasks* with *analytic rubrics* that allow students to self-assess and set goals. They create *activity sheets* that guide students through the day or week, listing the nonnegotiable teacher lessons, optional *small-group mini-lessons*, group activities, and individual activities. Students begin the day or week by designing a personalized schedule for their work. They monitor their progress and reflect on their work habits in journals. *How-to sheets* are available for students to use as they need to master a particular technology skill. They each keep their work in a two-pocket *student work folder* that holds completed and in-progress activities. Teachers become facilitators, moving around the classroom meeting with individual students and groups to guide learning. They carry grids or handheld computing devices to keep notes on student progress. They

---

* Reprinted from the IDEportal (www.ideportal.com) with permission.

review *student work folders* and make comments, set *small-group mini-lessons*, and set whole-class *benchmark lessons*.

These are just some of the structures that masterful teachers use to create a complex *scaffold for learning*. To see it in action in a classroom is to realize that the students take this scaffold for granted, feeling totally empowered to pursue their education and proud to take control, never realizing the incredible feat their teachers have accomplished in building it.

CREATE

You've designed a *problem-based task statement*, *analytic rubric*, and *scaffold for learning*. It's time to think about how that will play out in the classroom. As you read, keep a paper or digital journal of ideas you will want to implement. Take time to develop student materials to use in your classroom to build *student responsibility for learning*.

The Home Group

One structure for providing students with a sense of belonging is to assign them to a *home group*. I recommend groups of three or four students who will work together throughout the *ALU*, typically two to five weeks. Although the students will have collaborative responsibility for the final product, much of concept and skill building will take place on an individual basis. Consequently, it is unnecessary, and often unproductive, to establish groups of like-ability students. You do not want to create the academically challenged group and the gifted group. That being said, I would not recommend, at the beginning of the year, placing the most academically challenged student in the class in a group with the most gifted student. This situation could become frustrating for both at the start of learning to work in a *Learner-Active, Technology-Infused Classroom*. When designing the groups, seek to create a working mix of students in terms of achievement, gender, learning styles, personalities, and work habits. You'll want to spend a considerable amount of time on this: designing the lists, reviewing and modifying them, and perhaps returning to them the next day to ensure that the groups are well constructed.

The *home group* addresses the structures of taking responsibility for learning. Together, students discuss and plan out their time; they help one another find resources and make decisions about how to work; and they collaboratively assess progress. They also assist one another in mastering content, but the group's primary function is to provide each student with a sense of belonging to a group that collectively works together to accomplish a task. The *home group* is the first tier for assistance, shifting the power, if you will, away from being primarily with the teacher. Working in a group for an extended period of time allows students to build important twenty-first-century work skills in collaboration.

Switching groups for new *ALUs* offers students the experience of engaging more closely with many members of the class. Working as part of a group provides both comfort and challenges. Switching groups can minimize the amount of time a student must face any particular challenge when working with a group. For example, one group member might tend to take over the activities of the group. Although it's important for students to learn how to handle such peers, it's also pleasant to sometimes not have to deal with that particular challenge.

Some teachers like to allow students to create their own groups. This is possible after students learn how to work in a *home group* and understand how to best select group members. I would not recommend allowing students to establish their own groups until you are well-versed in running your *Learner-Active, Technology-Infused Classroom*.

Introducing the Problem-Based Task and Analytic Rubric

A well-crafted, authentic, open-ended, *problem-based task* should motivate students to learn—and learning is fun. Let me make a distinction here: Being *taught* is not always fun, but realizing you've accomplished something you could never do before is. I like to launch a new *problem-based task* with an opening reflection that usually consists of a three-minute period of thinking, drawing, or writing to focus students. For example, if I were going to introduce "The Airport Problem" (see Chapter 2), I might ask students to list what they know about airports or to brainstorm a list of adjectives that describe airports. The intent is to focus their minds, not to produce any sort of learning objective, so keep it short. This activity can be posted on the wall or classroom website as students enter the room at the beginning of a new unit, so they can get started while everyone settles into the classroom. In the case of the virtual classroom, you'd ask students to complete this reflection before watching the opening video.

Then as you bring the group together, you want to build their enthusiasm around the topic. Where possible, use world events, video, audio, and images to build a case for why you are presenting the question. This problem introduction should only take about ten minutes. Then hand out the *problem-based task* and *analytic rubric*. Ask students to read the task and then read down the *Practitioner* column of the rubric, circling or underlining everything they are going to need to learn to accomplish the task. Notice I did not say, "what they don't know." Focus on learning as a positive, productive experience rather than as a gap filler. You might want to have students offer up these statements of what they need to learn as a group, writing them or projecting them on the board. Then, let them know you've designed a lot of activities that will help them accomplish their goals. This process allows students to see what lies ahead and consider what they need to learn, thus taking responsibility for their own learning.

You may choose to assign students articles to read in advance of class to pique their interest in a topic. Then, the opening reflection might be relating their lives to the articles or generating questions from the articles. When you introduce the *problem-based task* and *analytic rubric*, students will already be motivated to complete it.

At this point, you're ready to hand out an *activity list* (more on that in a future section) and let them get started. Using these structures (the opening *benchmark lesson*, *problem-based task*, *analytic rubric*, and *activity list*) and strategies (having students reflect, presenting a case for the problem, having students read the *analytic rubric* on their own and consider what they need to learn), you will build *student responsibility for learning*.

Student Schedules

In the *Learner-Active, Technology-Infused Classroom*, students take responsibility for scheduling how they will use their time. You've developed a set of activities for your *problem-based task*, outlined in your *scaffold for learning*. The next step is to create a structure that allows your students to schedule how they will use their time. For primary-level students, I suggest beginning with scheduling a half-day of activities. Third-grade students and above can schedule a full day. In departmentalized settings, where class meets for a designated number of minutes each day, students can schedule across the week. For virtual courses, students should schedule a manageable amount of time allocated to work on the course content. The amount of forward-looking activities students can manage will depend upon their grade level, the amount of time they have experienced your *Learner-Active, Technology-Infused Classroom*, and the amount of years they've studied in such classrooms in the school.

I was redesigning a school one grade level at a time, beginning with fourth-grade classrooms. In the third year, I was talking with some of the sixth-grade students, asking them how the year was going. One boy said, "It's getting better. At first the teacher wouldn't let us schedule our own time, but we've been doing this for two years now. But she's catching on." The teacher was moving slowly because the idea of students managing their own time was new to her, but it wasn't new to her students.

To schedule time, students need an *activity list* and a blank schedule. The *activity list* is developed from the *scaffold for learning*. Primary students should be given a few activities to schedule across a half-day, giving them freedom to decide the order in which to accomplish them. For example, first-grade students might decide when to accomplish their buddy reading, journal writing, science experiment, and math worksheet. When they have mastered this scheduling skill, you can introduce choices, such as deciding between playing a math game, listening to a podcast, or attending a teacher-led lesson, all focusing on a single math skill.

By second grade, you can introduce the concept of scheduling start and stop times for activities. Although second graders are typically just learning to tell time, the promise of scheduling one's own time builds a *felt need* to learn to tell time. A group of teachers once told a colleague of mine that second graders were not developmentally ready to tell time. He suggested they provide students with the option of scheduling their own time if they can learn to read the clock. By October, all students were scheduling their day with varying degrees of teacher assistance. By December, the teachers presented students with a test that demonstrated that the students could tell time to the minute, at which point the teachers were dismayed to realize the state tests only require them to tell time at five-minute intervals. *Felt need* is a powerful motivator.

The importance of having students indicate start and end times for their planned activities cannot be overemphasized; it is the foundation of time management. If students merely determine the order in which they plan to complete activities, an activity that should require twenty minutes of attention could take forty minutes, and the student will be left believing that the teacher has assigned too much work. The *activity list* (Figure 6.1, page 92) designed by the teacher should indicate approximate completion times for activities, providing students with a self-assessment. If the *activity list* indicates that gathering and graphing the data should take thirty minutes, students who find themselves still collecting data at twenty minutes will know to seek additional instructional supports. By scheduling start and end times, students can reflect on their ability to work productively and schedule realistically: two important twenty-first-century skills.

In higher grades, students typically move from class to class according to some time period. Rather than scheduling vertically, that is, an entire day, students should schedule horizontally, that is, a week's worth of class periods. Mind you, if students are fortunate enough to be engaged in *Learner-Active, Technology-Infused Classrooms* throughout the day, they will end up scheduling both vertically and horizontally for the week. Even at the high school level, I do not recommend having students schedule out more than a week.

Figure 6.1. Sample Activity List

Radioactive Waste Smorgasbord
Activity List—Week 1

Required activities: Every student will complete these activities this week.

Name	Duration	Description
Settling Time Experiment	Group activity; allow approx. 20 minutes	How long will it take uraninite to settle to the bottom of a pond? This experiment will begin to build your knowledge in this area. Complete the experiment with one partner. We have two lab setups so you will need to sign up for a timeslot in advance.
Bacteria and Food	Individual activity; allow approx. 15 minutes	Visit the Virtual Museum of Bacteria website. Explore this site on how bacteria help us create and digest the food we eat.
Mystery Powder Experiment	Group activity; allow approx. 20 minutes	What's the difference between solution and suspension? Make observations during this experiment to understand a difference between uraninite and uranium.
Independent Research	Individual activity; time will vary from approx. 20 to 60 minutes	Use the Web to research what is known about bacteria, uranium, and the task at hand.

Choice Activities: Complete at least one of the following activities during this week.

Name	Duration	Description
Bacteria Basics	Individual activity; allow approx. 15 minutes	Read these textbook pages to familiarize yourself with bacterial characteristics.
Radioactive Waste is Delicious	Individual activity; allow approx. 20 minutes	A Web-based scavenger hunt on bacterial characteristics.
Berkeley's Bacteria page	Individual activity; allow approx. 20 minutes	Explore Berkeley's website on bacteria to explore bacterial characteristics.

Optional Activities: You may choose to complete these activities, or your teacher may assign them to you. These activities will supplement your core knowledge but will not be required of everyone completing the unit.

Name	Duration	Description
Radioactivity podcast	Individual or pairs activity; allow approx. 10 minutes	Learn more about the hazards of radioactivity by listening to this podcast.
Mini-Lesson	Individual activity; allow approx. 15 minutes	Attend the mini-lesson on bacterial metabolism to find out how bacteria get their energy.

The Activity List

The *activity list*, whether digital or on paper, should provide students with a reasonable number of activities to schedule over the course of the scheduling period (e.g., a half-day, day, or week). Each entry on the *activity list* should offer a brief description of the activity, indicate any prerequisites to tackling this activity, and provide an estimated timeframe for completion. I recommend grouping activities into three subheadings:

♦ *Required activities*—These include *benchmark lessons* and those activities that you want all students to complete.

♦ *Choice activities*—For any given skill or concept, offer students a variety of ways to build mastery, including those that address different cognitive levels, learning styles and intelligences, and disabilities. For example, offer a *small-group mini-lesson,* podcast, text selection, *how-to sheet,* interactive website, peer tutoring session, and hands-on activity. Students decide how many and which activities to schedule to build personal mastery.

♦ *Optional activities*—Most *problem-based tasks* lend themselves to many extensions and digressions. Optional activities allow students to pursue related interests. This is particularly useful for students who complete the main *problem-based task* and have the time to delve more deeply into areas of interest. For example, students who are focusing on a variety of grammatical rules may be given an activity of rewriting one grammar rule that they think should no longer apply in this day and age, explain why, and convince you that it would not adversely affect people's comprehension of text.

Although you still have control over the activities to be completed, students have the freedom to make choices as to how they will use their time and the resources they will use to meet your academic expectations. Depending on your comfort level, you might allow students to suggest other activities to add to the list. An ambitious student may, for example, locate instructional websites that are unknown to you.

Special education students with expressive processing issues may know what they want to do but lack the language to explain it. The *activity list* provides them with that language. For *problem-based tasks* that involve writing, the *activity list* becomes a "word wall" of sorts for terms students might need in their writing.

Teaching Students to Schedule Their Time

If you are teaching students that have previously attended classes in which the teacher tells them what to do and when to do it, scheduling their time will be an unfamiliar act. Sometimes, even the best activities, if unfamiliar, can cause students to be resistant. In this case, you'll want to ease students into scheduling. At first, provide them with a completely filled in schedule and let them know that you want them to be aware of the order in which you are going to offer and assign instructional activities. This schedule may, for example, indicate that you will start with a five-minute reflection written on the board, then offer a fifteen-minute lesson, have students complete a pairs activity for twenty minutes, and regroup for wrap up for five minutes.

After a few days at this level, you might introduce some flexibility. Tell your students that the order in which they complete two activities doesn't matter and allow them to fill in those blanks. Offer them choices as to three ways to accomplish the same learning and allow them to select the best fit for them. Keep in mind that if students attend your class or tackle a subject for forty-five minutes or less, you do not necessarily want to parse that time period into too many segments. Rather, you may have them schedule activities over two class periods. Twenty minutes is a good rule of thumb for the brain to remain engaged in an activity. Students who are engrossed in an activity may prefer to work for forty minutes; students who must accomplish a relatively simple task may need only ten minutes. Avoid, however, the temptation to divide the class period into three fifteen-minute segments asking students so switch activities every fifteen minutes. This approach could end up reducing productivity. The more fluid the schedule, the better.

Once you think students are succeeding at this level, open up the schedule even further and provide them with a primarily blank schedule, except for your required *benchmark lessons*, and allow them to complete the rest, referencing the *activity list*. It is important to then approve students' schedules, applying your insights into the project and students' work habits. You may recognize that a student has not allotted enough time to complete an activity or has selected an activity that is too easy or too hard. In these cases, advise the students accordingly.

Upon completing and implementing a schedule, students should reflect on their success. Ask students who did not complete their schedules to identify why. It may be that they did not schedule enough time. It may be that they were distracted. I observed a fourth-grade class in which students were brainstorming ideas for building a persuasive case. They were to cut the paper in a shape related to their topic and color in the edges. I watched as one group of students placed rulers on pencils to create whirligigs; one group spent a short period of time brainstorming and an inordinate amount of time coloring; one group stayed very focused and created an impressive list; and so forth. At the end of the activity, the teacher had students respond to a series of questions and assign themselves points for how well they accomplished their task. I was pleased to see how accurately the students assessed their work habits. The teacher ended by saying that the following day, she expected those groups that did not receive the highest score to modify their work habits toward greater success. Sure enough, students raised their performance level based on their reflections. It is important to *teach* students to manage their own time and to self-assess, rather than criticizing or attempting to control them.

One of the greatest frustrations I hear from teachers is the challenge of scheduling around all of the pullout programs. They believe that there is precious little time for them to have with the entire class. This is all the more reason to limit the amount of whole-class instruction in favor of providing learning activities for students to complete based on an individual schedule. If a *home group* includes a student who attends a replacement math class, then *that* group should schedule math at that time. That one students' schedule no longer affects the entire class and teacher.

Student Work Folders

Each student should have a physical or digital *student work folder* that remains in class. I suggest that in the case of a physical folder, you use a two-pocket folder labeled "Work in Progress" on one side and "Work Completed" on the other. In the case of a digital folder, you create subfolders into which students will place their work. When students arrive at class, they'll retrieve or open their *student work folders*, access their schedules, review any notes left by the teacher, and begin working. They'll move completed work that has been checked by the teacher out of the folder to take home. At the end of the class period, they'll ensure that their completed work is on one side, ready to be checked by the teacher. Managing papers or documents and categorizing work in progress from completed work will serve students well in their lives.

The Student Work Folder–Assessment Connection

Given that running a *Learner-Active, Technology-Infused Classroom* typically requires a series of paradigm shifts, let's look at the dominant paradigm for checking and grading student work. Teachers tend to have students hand papers in, grouped according to activity. If the goal is to make it easier for the teacher to grade papers, it makes sense to have stacks of papers for each assignment. The teacher then takes a stack of papers, turns to the answer key, and grades them.

Although this approach may optimize the teacher's time, it does little to improve student achievement. Raising student achievement requires the teacher to know the abilities of the student as a whole and plan for that student accordingly. When you open up a *student work folder*, you are seeing the student holistically. Consider a third-grade student: When you look at the folder, you see that she is strong in math skills but has difficulty with written expression. She seems to thrive on science and has strong observational skills, based on her drawings of science experiments. She has difficulty with map-reading skills. Consider a high school English student: His writing mechanics are strong; his writing is clear and well structured; his reading comprehension is below grade level; his ability to recognize figurative language is greatly lacking. The folder approach allows you to see and assess the student as a whole, providing you with insights into the student's overall ability and interests. In the case of the third grader, you might assign a writing assignment in which she describes what she observed in the science experiment. In the case of the high school English student, you might provide a figurative language *how-to sheet* and have him review a recent original story and embellish his writing.

During the course of the day, you may have met with the student and are therefore familiar with the contents of the folder. Generally, however, you'll want to check *student work folders* daily (for self-contained classes) or weekly (for departmentalized classes). You'll review each student's schedule, completed work, and work in progress. You'll make notes to the student and suggest other activities. You'll use the data you glean from the class set of *student work folders* to schedule benchmark and *small-group mini-lessons*.

It is important to instruct students to keep their *analytic rubrics* in their folders when they hand them in at the end of class. Additionally, they should indicate on the rubric what they have accomplished toward the *Practitioner* and *Expert* levels by checking off criteria. This way, you can see how students are progressing and make comments targeted to continued success.

Upon Entering the Classroom

Let's consider the moment when students enter the room. You want them to get started immediately, without any prompting from you. A common approach is to implement a "do now," but consider that a "do now" still has the teacher assigning the students work to do, and the level of responsibility does not move beyond following the teacher's directions. In taking a problem-based approach to instruction, you can have students schedule how to use their own time. At the most basic level, that involves asking students at the end of the day to identify what they should start working on the next day and then having them reference that note at the start of the next day. At a higher level, that involves having students map out how they are going to spend their time across a day or week. I address this in detail in the next few pages.

What administrative functions do you need to accomplish when students enter the room? Attendance? Lunch count? Collection of forms? Consider how you might accomplish this in ways that provide the students with the responsibility. Even kindergarten students can enter a classroom, find the clothespin or magnet with their name on it, and move it to the other side of a cabinet to indicate they are present. If students retrieve a physical folder or log onto a class website upon entering class, you'll easily be able to determine who is absent without calling names off of a roster and consuming precious instructional time. If students are assigned to *home groups*, you can have, for example, one student monitor attendance and lunch count and record that information to create a class compilation. Checklists posted on websites or physical classroom walls allow students to report in on issues such as lunch choices and field trip forms.

Analytic Rubrics

Analytic rubrics (see Chapter 3) allow students to self-assess and set goals. Key to using an *analytic rubric* to build *student responsibility for learning* is designing the rubric to drive instruction, rather than merely to evaluate the end product. *Analytic rubrics* designed to drive instruction offer students a clear path to success, introducing additional criteria in each column.

As you facilitate, expect your students to have their rubrics nearby with notes as to their progress. This might involve checking off a rubric box or highlighting criteria. As you sit with students, ask them to use the rubric to report on their progress and articulate their next steps.

A well-written *analytic rubric* will free a student to pursue learning independent of the teacher's prompting. For example, an *analytic rubric* involving graphing data may ask students to use a number line plot, histogram, box-and-whisker plot, stem-and-leaf plot, and scatter plot. The Novice column might require a number line plot; the Apprentice might require three or four of the five; the Practitioner column would require one of each. The student can easily begin to seek out resources for creating the graphs and check off those criteria that are satisfied. The student can then set a goal for mastering the next type of graph and locate the necessary instructional resources. The *analytic rubric* allows the student to take responsibility for learning.

The Resource Area

As students are working on their *problem-based tasks*, they will need a variety of resources, including *how-to sheets*; instructional podcasts, screencasts, and videocasts; articles; *analytic rubric*; activity direction sheets; and manipulatives. Typically, teachers hand out materials to students. If you hand out a direction sheet to your students and a student doesn't have one, whose responsibility is it? Yours. If you place the papers on a table and instruct students to retrieve them when they need them, and a student doesn't have the appropriate paper, whose responsibility is it? The student's. One teacher pointed out that homework completion increased once she placed the assignments in the *resource area*.

Establish an area to place materials that students will need. If your students all have personal computing devices, you might create a digital filing cabinet for files and links to websites. If not, create a physical space. This could be, for example, a table, a filing cabinet, a crate of folders, pockets on a bulletin board that can hold papers, or cubbyholes for tactile materials.

So as not to overwhelm students, it's a good idea to display the materials needed for the current set of activities in a prominent place in the *resource area* and avoid putting out materials to be used in the future. Materials used in the recent past that may need to remain for reference should be moved to a less prominent location in the *resource area*, such as the back of the table, or filed in a three-ring binder or file cabinet. Essentially, create an area where students can easily find what they need and not be distracted by materials they will need in the future.

A great tip for ensuring that you do not run out of paper copies is to write across the bottom copy, "Return to the Teacher," highlighted, so that the student who finds only that copy on the table takes it to the teacher to indicate the need for additional copies.

The Help Board

As students begin working on the various activities toward the accomplishment of the *problem-based task*, you will facilitate instruction by moving around the room and sitting with a student or group for a few minutes. It would be extremely disruptive for students to be calling out for help. You want your facilitation to be proactive and not reactive.

Teach your students that their first line of help is their *home group*. If they don't understand a direction, are not sure where to find a resource, or need help understanding a concept or skill, they should seek out a *home group* member first, then approach other students. If students need *your* help, they should write their names on the *help board*. This can be a space on a whiteboard, a paper on a bulletin board, or a digital comment on a Web-based help page.

The *help board* meets the needs of both the students and the teacher. While facilitating, teachers need to know who is in need of more immediate guidance. When the teacher is meeting with students, other students are not supposed to interrupt. They can, however, add their name to the *help board* to indicate their need. Often students write their names on the *help board* and then erase them, having found alternate ways to answer their questions.

As a teacher, your job is to keep an eye on the *help board* and provide assistance in a timely manner. When you finish facilitating with a group, check the *help board*. In the *Learner-Active, Technology-Infused Classroom*, you're not teaching lessons and then letting students work independently, in which case they would most likely require little of your attention. Rather, they are engaged in challenging learning experiences and you are teaching as you facilitate those experiences. Address those who need help in a reasonable period of time; however, teach your students to begin working on another activity if they find themselves stuck. No one should ever be simply waiting for the teacher; they should move on to another, less-challenging, activity while waiting.

The Quality Work Board

Teachers often use subjective words such as neat, descriptive, complete, and compelling when describing expectations. What does "neat" look like? It helps for students to see examples of high-quality work to gain a better understanding of expectations and to clarify any subjectivity. If you teach in your own classroom, you might use a bulletin board area for this. If you move from classroom to classroom throughout the day, consider a three-ring binder. If every student in your classroom has a mobile computing device, consider a digital folder or website.

You can hang student work from previous years; and you can hang your own examples. If you want students, for example, to draw their observations of plant growth, you might draw a diagram of a sliced-open piece of fruit, labeling the parts, and including anything you think makes a neat, complete, observational drawing. That way, you are showing an example of drawing from observation without doing the assignment for them. I suggest posting quality work without names, and I often refrain from posting work completed by students in the class. The point is not to create competition as much as it is to demonstrate what quality work looks like.

Obviously, quality work goes beyond those items that can be posted on a bulletin board. What do strong oratory skills sound like? What does a powerful song sound like? What does a well-crafted piece of pottery look like? Be creative! With today's technology, you can capture video and audio and post it to a digital folder. You can videotape yourself holding a piece of pottery and pointing out what makes it quality work.

Table Journals

One way to focus students on the effectiveness of their *home group* is with a *table journal*. At the end of a session during which students are working together as a group, have them spend a couple of minutes reflecting on their effectiveness using a set of questions or indicators. The reflection can be different from day to day, but the goal is the same: Have students assess how effective and productive they are and what they can do to become more effective and productive. The indicators will differ, depending on the age of the students, and will become more sophisticated over the course of the school year to build greater collaborative skills.

A *table journal* can be created as a digital or paper document. Figures 6.2 and 6.3 (page 102) offer some examples of *table journal* pages.

Resource Signup Sheets

You will most likely have some limited resources in the *Learner-Active, Technology-Infused Classroom*, for example: microscopes set up to view cells, computers, reading center, listening center, soundproof studio room, and *learning centers*. The key is that not all students can access the resource at the same time. Resource signup sheets coupled with student scheduling allows students to make use of limited resources easily. Many schools attempt to outfit classrooms with full sets of resources. An advantage of the *Learner-Active, Technology-Infused Classroom* is that you can save money on such resources because you don't have to purchase an entire class set. You can provide students with more diverse offerings if you are willing to have students engaged in various activities at the same time; that is, giving up overt control in return for a structured environment in which students take charge of their learning.

As with all situations in the *Learner-Active, Technology-Infused Classroom*, you want to figure out how to build *student responsibility for learning* rather than overtly controlling the limited resources. Use a signup process. If you have a limited number of computers in the room, post a signup sheet with timeslots, allowing a student to sign up, for example, for only one slot per day. As students schedule the day or week, they determine when resources are available, sign up at the location of the resource, and indicate the time they will be using it on their schedule.

Figure 6.2. Table Journal: Example 1

Table Journal

Each group member should rank the following statements on a scale of 1 to 5, with 1 being the lowest score and 5 being the highest. Rank independently. Then one person should record the results of the group by marking how many members rated each statement with a 1, 2, 3, 4, or 5. Be honest in your assessment!

	1	2	3	4	5
The group arrived and got started immediately without any prompting from the teacher.					
The group involved everyone in all aspects of the work, but still divided responsibilities.					
Every member of the group participated throughout the work session.					
All members were encouraged to voice their opinions.					
The group worked through conflicts by discussing options and reaching consensus.					
Group members used their time well.					

Discuss how you might work even better as a group the next time and record ideas here:

Figure 6.3. Table Journal: Examples 2 and 3

Table Journal

As a group, discuss how you have worked differently as a group today as compared to prior days. What have you learned about working in a group.

Table Journal

This is it: Your last chance to reflect on your work as a group! What was most effective about your group during this problem-based unit?

How might your group have been even more effective?

If you were to give other students advice on working well as a group, what would it be?

Remember the seventh-grade science teacher from Chapter 1? He instructed his students to view a video and make a paper airplane by a certain date. They then signed up for timeslots to utilize the video station and he didn't need to be involved. I watched a first-grade teacher in a morning class meeting describe the various *learning centers* students could use right after lunch. Each station had two cardboard pockets next to it. Students had cards with their names on them. When the meeting was over, they calmly walked around the room and selected one center to use that afternoon. In this case, they had to make a decision and sign up in advance to use a *learning center*. If a peer already selected that center, they had to select another and wait for another day to use the desired center. The key is to find a way to have your students sign up for the use of limited resources.

This structure applies to your time as well. Limit the amount of one-on-one conferences you have with students; they keep you from the rest of the class. However, if you are planning to meet with individual students or groups of students, create a sign-up sheet and have them select a timeslot. It's a good idea to leave open time between conferences so that you can circulate the room to engage with students, and see whose names are on the *help board*.

Small-Group Mini-Lesson Signup

As a differentiation structure, the *small-group mini-lesson* allows you to provide a short (five- to ten-minute) lesson to a small group of students (no more than six) who are ready to learn a particular skill at the same time. As a *student responsibility for learning* structure, it allows students to self-assess whether or not they should attend the lesson and then sign up for it. Here are some more tips for engaging students as active participants:

♦ Provide the tools for students to self-assess to determine if they should attend the lesson. These might include quizzes, checklists, pretests, and a sct of questions.

♦ Announce *small-group mini-lessons* well enough in advance for students to consider them when scheduling their time. That might be the day before or the beginning of the week. From time to time you will find the need to add a lesson unexpectedly, based on your formative assessments, and students will have to adjust their schedules. But this should be the exception to the norm.

♦ To announce the lessons, post them on a specific area on the board, bulletin board, classroom website, or other online venue. Include the start time and length of the lesson so that students can schedule accordingly.

♦ Offer students options for learning the content other than attending the lesson. Students may be inclined to think the only way to learn is by listening to you in person. Only you can dispel that myth. Offer clearly written *how-to sheets*, podcasts, websites, models, and other means of learning the content so that only those who truly need to be in attendance are at the lesson.

♦ Do not waver from your group size limit. Allow students to sign up for the lesson or, if all of the slots are filled, add their name to an overflow list so that you will offer a second session. If you have too many overflow situations, you probably need to focus your lessons more. For example, a *small-group mini-lesson* on "Writing a Thesis Statement" may be too broad. Rather, try "Getting Started with Writing a Thesis Statement" (for those who have no idea how to write a thesis statement) and "Making Your Thesis Statement More Powerful" (for those who believe they can write a thesis statement but are unsure of how good it is). Focusing more specifically on content will ensure students are at the lesson that fits their needs and that you will not be conducting the same lesson repeatedly.

♦ Stick to your timeslots. Begin and end *small-group mini-lessons* on time. Otherwise, the scheduling becomes compromised and your class will not run as smoothly. If you find a topic warrants more time, schedule a followup lesson.

RECAP

Engaging students in the learning process includes employing a variety of structures and strategies to create greater *student responsibility for learning*. As you design your *ALU* and learning environment, be sure to include the following:

♦ Home group designations for students to have a sense of belonging and a first tier of support in their work

♦ A compelling opening to the ALU that inspires and motivates students

♦ Student scheduling of how they will use their time

♦ Activity lists to guide student scheduling

♦ A plan for teaching students how to schedule their time

♦ Student work folders

♦ A resource area

♦ A help board

♦ A quality work board

♦ Table journals

♦ Resource signup sheets

♦ *Small-group mini-lessons* signup sheets

7

Facilitating Learning

You walk into a classroom to find students actively engaged in diverse activities, clearly attending to the tasks at hand. The teacher is sitting and talking with a student. After a few minutes, the teacher moves to sit with a group of students. Again, after a few minutes, the teacher moves to sit with another student. At some point, you ask the teacher to tell you about a particular student. With ease, the teacher tells you what the student is working on, how he is progressing in his learning goals, where his challenges are, and what the teacher plans to do to address them. How is the teacher able to do this with so much activity in the classroom? The answer lies in masterful facilitation of the learning environment, the subject of this chapter. I frequently use the following GPS metaphor to shed light on the teacher's role as facilitator of learning.

Teacher as GPS*

Global Positioning Systems (GPSs) are becoming increasingly popular, particularly in cars for assisting the driver in meeting a destination. Did you ever stop to consider that a masterful teacher is a lot like GPS?

First, the GPS identifies the destination. A teacher identifies the destination as the curriculum standards that the students need to meet. Next, the GPS determines the best route for the driver to use to meet the destination. A teacher creates lesson plans and activities that are expected to help the student achieve the curricular goals.

During the trip, the GPS continually uses satellite communications to determine where the driver is. Based on that information and the destination, GPS ensures that the driver is "on track" to meet the destination. If the driver makes an incorrect turn, the

---

* Reprinted from the IDEportal (www.ideportal.com) with permission.

GPS immediately recognizes that and develops a new plan for ensuring the driver arrives at the destination.

Masterful teachers use continual assessments to determine students' progress and then modify lessons and activities to ensure student success. Quizzes, rubrics, verbal check-ins, gathering facilitation data, online assessments, and the like enable the teacher to track the progress of each student. If a student is having difficulty with a previously taught lesson, the teacher will meet one-on-one or in small groups, utilize a technology program, develop a "how-to" sheet, or use some other means to ensure that the student masters the skill or concept.

Of course, another wonderful aspect of GPS is that it never makes you feel like a failure. At each wrong turn, it merely recalculates the route. My GPS has never told me, "That's it! I'm not going to help you any more if you're not going to listen to my directions!" or "You just really don't have what it takes to get to your destination." On the contrary, my GPS always instills in me great confidence that I will arrive at my destination, as do masterful teachers.

CONSIDER

Facilitating learning presumes that the teacher has already set up clear structures for a learning environment, as discussed in the previous chapters, and students are now engaged in the learning process. In a more conventional model of teaching, the teacher presents information to the entire class, typically from the front of the room, and then students engage in practicing what was presented. The teacher need only walk around the room to ask if students need help, as they are already armed with content from the lesson. In the *Learner-Active, Technology-Infused Classroom*, this is not the case. Students are learning in a differentiated environment in which content is presented in a variety of ways, rarely through the teacher in the front of the room. Therefore, the role of the teacher as facilitator during this time becomes critical. It is not enough to ask if students need help, as they may not know that they even *need* help. Facilitation in the *Learner-Active, Technology-Infused Classroom* falls into four categories:

- Asking logistical questions to guide students' efforts.

- Asking probing questions to stimulate higher-order thinking.

- Using formative assessments to track student progress in terms of content mastery.

♦ Tracking formative assessment data and using it to drive instructional decisions.

Clearly, when you are offering *benchmark lessons* or *small-group mini-lessons*, you are "on stage" in front of the entire class or a small group of students. Beyond that time, you should be engaged as a facilitator. It's important to resist the temptation to think that students are well engaged and you can grade papers, plan lessons, or talk at length with a visitor to the classroom. Your facilitation time is a critical part of the teaching process.

As students are engaged in the learning process, you need to be moving around the room, pulling up a chair to sit with one or a group of students. "Never hover!" Again, if you only had to ask if students needed help, you could lean over their desks. If you are going to engage with them in the learning process in a meaningful way, you should be seated alongside them.

James Coleman (1988) introduced the term *social capital* to mean that which is produced as a result of powerful relationships between adults and young people in a community. In a nutshell, consider a community in which the parents know the youngsters in the neighborhood by name, congratulate them for a sports win, offer a ride home from school, ask about an ill parent, and so forth. In such communities, students build confidence and are secure in the knowledge that there are adults who are interested in them. In such communities, students tend to fare well in school. Juxtapose that with a community in which the adults do not know the neighborhood youngsters and are not concerned about them. Students are left to fend for themselves with little formal or informal adult supervision. In such communities, students tend to fare poorly in school. Coleman's work in defining social capital has led large, urban schools to restructure into small learning communities (SLCs). In the *Learner-Active, Technology-Infused Classroom*, it reminds teachers that those critical, caring relationships between adults and students are best fostered during one-on-one and small-group facilitation.

Be mindful of your time as you move about the room, spending only a few minutes at each stop. Although at times you will be tempted to engage in lengthy conversation with one or more students, consider that you would then be absent from the rest of the class. You might suggest that you and the student meet again to continue the discussion at a specified time. You may decide to conduct a related *small-group mini-lesson*.

CREATE

So far, you've developed a *problem-based task, analytic rubric, scaffold for learning*, and *activity list*. Once all this learning activity gets underway, you'll want to rely on your facilitation tools to gather formative assessment data to drive your instructional decisions. Avoid relying solely on your intuition, observations, or memory—gather the data!

Asking Logistical Questions

Building greater *student responsibility for learning* involves expecting students to self-assess, make decisions about which activities to choose and when to complete them, select instructional resources, and make many other decisions. Part of the facilitation process is ensuring that students are carrying out these tasks successfully. When facilitating and sitting with students, ask them to show you where they are on their *analytic rubrics* for the *problem-based task*. Ask them what their next step is going to be and why? Ask how they decided upon the activities they've chosen. Ask how they will know when they've accomplished the next column in the rubric. Ask them if they are attending a particular *small-group mini-lesson,* and why or why not. Ask them how they decided upon the resources they've selected.

These types of questions will help you feel confident in their decision making and will model for them the types of internal conversations they should be having surrounding their learning decisions. The more you teach your students how to take responsibility for decisions in the learning process, the more time you can spend on content mastery as opposed to logistics. You don't want to be the teacher reading off names to check whether or not students completed their homework. You don't want to be the teacher who asks students to put their homework on their desks and then walks around with a grade book recording the presence of homework. You don't want to be the teacher who is reprimanding individual students for not being on task or for not following directions. All of these actions take precious time away from what you do best: impart knowledge to your students and help them become lifelong learners. Have students self-report on homework. If they are inaccurately reporting, you'll know it from their performance and can talk with them about the importance of and your expectation for accurate reporting. The more you create structures that allow students to take responsibility for logistics, the more time you'll have to spend on content, which will have a direct, positive impact on achievement.

Asking Probing Questions

Consider the following examples. A teacher meets with an eighth-grade student who summarizes a section of text. The teacher asks, "How does the author's word choice create the mood?" This question causes the student to delve more deeply into the text, focusing on word choice and the literary element of mood. A fifth-grade student exploring space suggests NASA should fly a manned spaceship to Mars in search of water. The teacher points out that a serious obstacle is the amount of radiation between the Earth and Mars and its potential disastrous effects on the astronauts. Assuming this is new information to the student, it will put her mind in motion thinking about where the radiation is coming from and how to overcome that obstacle. A kindergarten student brings in a collection of fall leaves and classifies them according to color. The teacher asks, "Can you classify them according to the type of edges?" This challenge pushes the student to focus on a more subtle feature of leaves than color.

When facilitating, most teachers tend to ask comprehension questions to ensure that students have a grasp on the basic content. Educational psychologist Benjamin Bloom worked with colleagues in the 1950s to develop a classification for intellectual activities inherent in the learning process. Bloom acknowledged that first someone must be able to *recall* information, then *comprehend* it, then *apply* it to various situations, then *analyze* it, which leads to the ability to *synthesize* and thus the create new information, and finally *evaluate* the creation of new information. Bloom's Taxonomy remains a viable guide for teachers when considering learning activities. You can also use it when considering the types of questions to ask students to probe their thinking. Some fifty years later, a student of Bloom's, Lorin Anderson (2001), updated the original taxonomy, primarily flipping the order of the last two categories (Figure 7.1).

Figure 7.1. Bloom's Taxonomy Updated

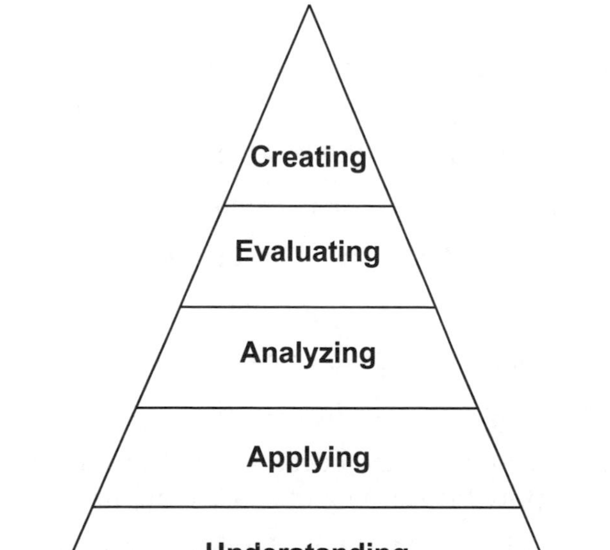

In the *Learner-Active, Technology-Infused Classroom*, teachers essentially ask five types of questions, somewhat mirroring Bloom's Taxonomy, though not entirely:

♦ Comprehension questions to assess students' understanding of content, and thus also recall.

♦ Application questions to assess students' ability to apply learning to new situations.

♦ Connection questions to assess students' ability to connect learning to their lives.

♦ Synthesis questions to encourage students to create new information from existing data.

♦ Metacognitive questions to prompt students to think about their own learning processes.

Used in combination, these questions probe students thinking.

While you will certainly have many questions in your mind to ask students during a unit of study, it's important to think through specific questions that correspond to each of five levels.

1. *Comprehension Questions*—It is important to ask questions that ensure students understand the content and skills needed to solve the problem. Examples:

   a. What do you need to do to accomplish this task? (To determine the student's understanding of the problem.)

   b. What did the Colonists think of the Stamp Act?

   c. What is the formula to calculate the area of a square?

   d. What do human beings need to survive?

   e. How can you find that information on the Internet?

   f. What type of graph will you make to display the data?

   g. What is the definition of an adjective?

2. *Application Questions*—Ask questions that ensure the ability of students to apply the learning to new situations.

   a. How do you think Martin Luther King, Jr. would respond to the move to eliminate affirmative action quotas from college admissions departments?

   b. What is the area of *this* classroom?

c. In what ways would human beings on Earth have to evolve to live on Mars?

d. What are at least ten adjectives you could use to describe this room?

3. *Connection Questions*—Ask questions that ensure the ability of students to apply learning to their lives.

   a. What skills learned here could you use in other places outside of school?

   b. How did Martin Luther King, Jr.'s work affect your life?

   c. Who do you know who was an adult during the Civil Rights movement whom you might e-mail for more information?

   d. Under what circumstances would you be ready to live on Mars?

   e. What are at least ten adjectives you could use to describe yourself?

4. *Synthesis Questions*—Ask questions that encourage students to create new information from existing data.

   a. What might the Civil Rights movement for the twenty-first century be?

   b. Given the formula for surface area of a plane surface, how might you determine the formula for surface area of a curved surface?

   c. What predictions might you make for temperature trends in January for the northeastern United States over the next 100 years?

   d. What capability do you think computers will possess in the next twenty years that they do not now possess?

   e. What will you write to persuade your audience to take your advice?

5. *Metacognition Questions*—Ask questions that prompt students to think about their own thinking processes.

   a. What was the hardest part of this task for you?

   b. How did you arrive at the solution?

   c. What did you think when your line of logic no longer made sense?

d. How might you go about solving this differently?

e. How did you figure out how to change the color combinations in this graph?

f. What problems did you encounter while creating this animated sequence and how did you solve them?

Take time to write up at least five questions for each of the above levels related to the authentic learning unit (*ALU*) you are designing. When you finish, reread them and see if you can improve upon them. Once you've designed them, you typically don't need to carry them with you while facilitating. Conversations with students will spark your memory.

Using Formative Assessments to Drive Instruction

A GPS is constantly sending out satellite signals to determine the progress of the driver and modify the route if necessary. Masterful teachers use formative assessment constantly to determine how students are progressing. This is a key paradigm shift in the *Learner-Active, Technology-Infused Classroom:* Teachers do not take comfort in the fact that they presented the content well; they only take comfort in the evidence that students learned the content well.

I heard a great analogy that states: formative assessment is to summative assessment as a physical is to an autopsy. Summative assessments are administered at the end of a unit of study or year in school to evaluate the level of success of the student. The understanding is that the teaching–learning process for this content is completed. The best information a summative assessment can offer the teacher relative to improving student achievement is in helping the teacher rethink the unit for the next group of students. Similarly, an autopsy will do nothing for the person being autopsied; however, the data can be used to advance the future of medicine. Alternatively, a physical is meant to assess the patient's condition and lead to prescribed actions aimed at improving patient health. Likewise, formative assessments are intended to provide data that will be used to prescribe learning activities that will lead to greater student success.

Formative assessments can be classified as follows: temperature gauges, breakpoints, student-directed assessments, and comprehensive assessments (Figure 7.2).

Consider these four categories and design assessments that you will use with your students.

1. *Temperature Gauges*—When you are presenting to the whole class, it's easy to take your cues from the handful of students who are smiling, nodding, and answering and asking questions. It's important not to be lulled into thinking this means your lesson is ef-

Figure 7.2. Four Types of Formative Assessment

♦ Temperature Gauges—Immediate, in-the-moment assessments that allow the teacher to get a sense of current student status.

Based on student response, the teacher can adjust lesson content and pace, and identify any urgent student needs.

Examples: Adjective Check-in, 3-Finger Check-in

♦ Breakpoints—Brief assessments given at a stopping point in instruction, allowing the teacher to step back and revise the instructional plan.

Based on student response, the teacher can offer targeted small group instruction, differentiated learning activities, and adapt benchmark lessons.

Examples: Exit Cards, One-Sentence Summary, Do Now, Higher-Order Questioning, Quizzes

♦ Student Directed Assessments—Self-evaluative student reflection, giving the teacher insight into perceived needs.

Based on student response, the teacher can provide resources such as instruction, websites, learning activities, and *how-to sheets*.

Examples: Checklists, Self-Assessment on a Rubric, Peer Evaluation, Student Journals

♦ Comprehensive Assessments—Systematic data collection on individual skill and concept attainment.

Based on student response, the teacher can offer targeted small-group instruction, reteach core concepts, and provide additional resources.

Examples: Rubrics, Tests, *Facilitation Grids*, Individual Conferences/Oral Interviews, *Student Folders*, Notebook/Portfolio Check

fective for the entire class. A quick check-in will provide you with important data. If you're talking about nutrition, for example, you can use a couple of temperature gauges. You can ask for a three-finger check-in: "Tell me how you're doing. Raise one finger if you're not yet sure of the food groups, two fingers if you can name most of them, three fingers if you can name all the food groups and give an example of each." Some teachers believe that students will not be honest if others are looking on, so they begin with, "Eyes closed." I'm assuming I need not go into the danger of "finger" check-ins with middle-grade students. This formative assessment tool must be carefully explained in advance; that is, which finger to raise if you're just raising one finger, etc. You could also use a thumb-up, thumb-down signal. If you're introducing a unit of study and have just handed out the *problem-based task*, *analytic rubric*, and *activity list*; you may want to see how students are feeling. Use the adjective check-in to have each student offer one word of how they are feeling. You'll hear words like interested, excited, confused, and overwhelmed. This allows you to get a read on the class. If you have a lot of students who are confused and overwhelmed, offer a *small-group mini-lesson* directly after the *benchmark lesson* for those who want to ask more clarifying questions and get more assistance before diving in. Keep in mind that students have to get used to these Temperature Gauge formative assessments. At first you might not get data as accurate as you want. Over time, students will realize this is critical feedback they are providing that is going to benefit them, and they will respond accordingly. The purpose of a Temperature Gauge is to provide you with the data to shift the focus of your lesson immediately. If you've just introduced the concept of foreshadowing, offer a three-finger check-in on whether or not a student could give an example of foreshadowing. If you find that few can provide one, you'll want to rethink your approach and offer perhaps some more examples.

2. *Breakpoints*—At the end of a day, class period, or whole- or small-group lesson, take the opportunity to gather assessment data. An exit card offers students a single, short question or request for information. The students write on an index card and hand it in on their way out the door or upon leaving the lesson. If students are working on a variety of activities around biomes and habitats, ask them to list something they learned today, or ask them to list a biome that interests them and why. Avoid closed-ended questions such as "list the major biomes," as, given that exit cards are completed as students are packing up or transitioning, students might simply ask a peer for the answer. Quizzes are also Breakpoint assessments. At the end of the day or class period, you might offer a ten-question quiz to assess learning. The key to Breakpoint assessments is that they offer you valuable data to use to plan subsequent lessons, offering you more time to adjust than a Temperature Gauge assessment does.

3. *Student-Directed Assessments*—These are powerful because they not only provide you with information, but they force students to become aware of their own progress. Prior to handing in an assignment, have students complete a checklist to ensure they've included all of the learning objectives you expected. A reflective portfolio allows students to set goals, gather examples of progress, reflect on them, and share their insights with you. Sit with individual students and ask them to use the unit rubric to tell you where they are in their progress and how they are going to move to the next column. Student-Directed Assessments tend to take a little more time than the previous two categories, but they provide valuable data about the students' perceptions of their learning as well as data on their actual progress.

4. *Comprehensive Assessments*—Not to be confused with summative assessments, Comprehensive Assessments gather data across a variety of concepts and skills. Rubrics are one example as they contain indicators for all aspects of the unit performance. *Facilitation grids* gather data from across a set of concepts and skills. These allow you to get the big picture of how the unit itself is progressing so that you can provide clarifying information and new instructional activities as needed. In order to meet overall curriculum standards for the year, an *ALU* can only be allocated a specific amount of time. Even if students are thoroughly engaged in a particular unit, you cannot afford to let it simply continue, as you have other units to launch. If students are not progressing adequately, Comprehensive Assessments will make that obvious, allowing you to provide additional information on a classroom blog or website; offer some targeted *benchmark lessons* or *small-group mini-lessons*; or modify some activities or add new ones.

Formative Assessment Grids

The beauty and challenge of the *Learner-Active, Technology-Infused Classroom* is the level of activity going on in the classroom at any one time. A common fear of teachers is tracking classroom activity: How are you going to track everything that is going on? Two very effective tools are the *task management grid* and the *content facilitation grid*. These grids enable you to easily track and analyze assessment data. Both can be designed on a spreadsheet or with a table in a word processing document. Both can be invaluable when speaking with parents, colleagues, and students about academic progress.

Task Management Grid

The *task management grid* allows you to easily see which activities a single student or the class has completed. Across the top are the various activities presented to students; down the left side are the students' names. To design your *task management grid*, consider the various subtasks students will accomplish to complete the problem. What assignments will students hand in? You may choose to include all of the learning activities you've assigned to build to each of the subtasks. For example, you may have students researching a topic and writing a persuasive letter. Figure 7.3 is a sample *task management grid* for writing a persuasive letter. Once students have researched the topic, they will hand in note cards for you to grade. Then they will hand in a graphic organizer for you to grade. In this case, the *task management grid* includes all of the handed-in or graded assignments. For students who need more direction, you might include more of the activities listed on the grid, not all of which will necessarily be graded. Use whatever system works best for you in tracking each students' activities.

Figure 7.3. Task Management Grid

	Note Cards	Graphic Organizer	Persuasive Techniques Plan	Draft Letter	Peer Editing w\ 2 Students	Final Copy
Alicia Capstone						
Jamal Jackson						
Joshua Morgan						
Trent Wade						

√ = Completed   S = Submitted   R = Return for Revisions

Reviewing students' folders will give you an idea of how well they are progressing in the curricular content, but it's not always easy to see which activities have been completed. The *task management grid* allows you to glance across a row to see how productive a student is. It also allows you to identify very popular activities (those completed by many students early on) and unpopular activities (those that remain incomplete for a long time). Some teachers hang a large poster board *activity list* on the wall so that students can check off their progress. Although not assessing success in content mastery, it will provide you with data that you can use to guide students. Those who may have completed a lot of activities may not be spending enough time grappling with the content to receive the benefit of the activities. In this case, you'll want to slow them down and perhaps ask them to complete a reflection card or a learning journal on what they learned. Students who are not completing enough may need assistance in scheduling their time or on content mastery itself. You might want to encourage some of these students to sign up for a *small-group mini-lesson* with you to build scheduling skills.

Content Facilitation Grid

Perhaps the most important tool for using formative assessment to drive instruction is the *content facilitation grid*. When students are working and you are not offering a *benchmark lesson* or *small-group mini-lesson*, you should be facilitating learning. The *content facilitation grid* is similar in structure to the *task management grid* except that, instead of activities across the top, you enter concepts and skills (Figures 7.4, page 118, and 7.5, page 119). As you pull up a chair next to a student or group of students, you'll be gathering valuable assessment data. Use the grid to make notations. For example, it you see evidence that a student has mastered a skill, write an "M" in that part of the grid. If a student has not only mastered the skill or concept but can explain it to another, use "P" for peer expert. If a student seems to have an adequate knowledge base but you feel could use some practice, use "HW" to indicate that you should assign a specific homework assignment on that skill. "ML" indicates the student needs help and should attend a *small-group mini-lesson*.

Given that an *ALU* spans several weeks and involves a number of concepts and skills, it's best to design separate *content facilitation grids* for each week. You might want to carry them on a clipboard with the current one on top or use a handheld computing device with digital grids. Most of the data you'll be collecting will be from the current week's grid, however, sometimes you'll need to refer to past or future grids.

In addition to making notations while moving around the room, you can also use the *facilitation grid* to track assessment data when reviewing student work. As you review *student folders*, you can add notations under specific skills and concepts. I caution you against using homework to make notations regarding mastery as you cannot always determine how much help the student may have received at home. You could use a small check or slash to indicate the student completed homework on the concept or skill and still add an assessment notation later.

(Text continues on page 120.)

Figure 7.4. Content Facilitation Grid

	Plot a point given the coordinate pair	Identify the coordinate pair given a plotted point	Draw a line segment given two coordinate pairs	Draw a line given a linear equation	Explain "slope of a line"	Identify the slope of the line using the graph	Calculate the slope of the line using two points	Explain where one might use the slope of a line in real life
Sarah Abington								
Mike Arturo								
Leah Brooks								
Brianna Caplan								

M = mastery   P = peer expert level   HW = needs homework for reinforcement
W = working on it   ML = needs a mini-lesson

Figure 7.5. A Global Solution Content Facilitation Grid

	Glaciers			Global Warming					Recommendations				Usage		
	Describes a glacier	Describes the environment in which glaciers are found	Examines the importance of glaciers on Earth	Describes global warming	Analyzes the major causes of global warming	Explains the climatic impact of global warming on glaciers	Explains the economic impact	Explains the environmental impact	Analyzes the Clean Air Act	Makes suggestions regarding global warming and glaciers	Bases recommendations on scientific evidence	Explains impact recommendations would have on glaciers	Uses scientific vocabulary and information	Clear, engaging and detailed	Demonstrates scientific writing process
Ashton, Carl															
Azul, Benita															
Barry, Janis															
Copeland, Sky															
Diaz, Raul															
Fields, Kevin															
Gallo, Abbie															

M = mastery   P = peer expert level   HW = needs homework for reinforcement   W = working on it   ML = needs a mini-lesson

As the *content facilitation grid* fills up, you can use it to assess students' progress and your own effectiveness. By looking horizontally, across a row, you can assess how an individual student is progressing on content mastery. This allows you to encourage a student to complete specific activities or attend specific *small-group mini-lessons*, assign homework, meet with the student to explain content, arrange for a *peer expert* session, and so forth.

By looking vertically, down a concept or skill column, you can assess your own success in designing the learning environment. If many students are having difficulty with a particular skill, you will want to rethink how you're delivering the instruction. You may need additional activities, a different explanation, an additional *small-group mini-lesson*, and so forth.

To get started, think through the concepts and skills students must master in this unit. Be sure that you are specific enough that you can assess a student effectively. For example, "knows parts of speech" could be an appropriate skill set for a sixth-grade student, but for a fourth-grade student, you would probably want to use one column for each part of speech and enter the description as "defines, can recognize, and can use nouns."

You might want to highlight initial columns you consider to be prerequisite skills. That way, you know that most students should be able to easily demonstrate mastery of those skills, with the unit concepts and skills beginning in subsequent columns. See the *problem-based tasks* in the Appendices for sample *content facilitation grids*.

It is important that you *use* formative assessment data daily. As a result of this data, you should make adjustments to the instructional activities you are offering. You'll want to allocate time to review each *student folder* and the *facilitation grids* in order to write a note to an individual student, providing direction for future activities.

RECAP

In the *Learner-Active, Technology-Infused Classroom*, teachers thoughtfully plan for the use of deliberate and purposeful structures and strategies to facilitate instruction. Review the follow list to ensure that you have a plan for each in your *ALU*:

♦ Ask logistical questions about the student's goals, schedule, resource choices, activity completion, rubric progress, etc.

♦ Ask probing questions to push higher-order thinking, beginning with comprehension questions and then moving to application, connection, synthesis, and metacognition. Brainstorm questions in advance so they'll come to use easily during the facilitation process.

♦ Plan for a variety of daily, formative assessments, including temperature gauges, breakpoints, student directed, and comprehensive.

♦ Use a *task management grid* to track students' progress in completing activities.

♦ Use *content facilitation grids* to track students' progress in mastering concepts and skills.

♦ Use the data gleaned from the *content facilitation grids* to schedule *small-group mini-lessons* and modify the unit's *activity list*.

8

Physical Classroom Design

The "Big Room" was a collaborative effort among three teachers who taught fifth grade. Based on their school's structure, the teachers taught their homeroom students language arts literacy, and then each of the three teachers taught all of the students either math, science, or social studies. Students moved from one class to the other throughout the day, sharing three teachers, as an introduction to greater departmentalization that was to come in subsequent years. My colleagues and I had been working in the school for three years, designing *Learner-Active, Technology-Infused Classrooms*, after which time these three teachers approached me indicating that they finally "got it" and wanted to run an amazing classroom by taking down the walls between the classrooms. I spoke with the superintendent, who had a knack for supporting teachers with great ideas, and he had the impeding wall taken down.

That summer, the teachers and I brainstormed, designed, and prepared for the fall, incorporating a lot of paradigm shifting. I questioned whether every student needed a seat facing the front of the room. If sometimes students are in their seats, sometimes at a computer, sometimes conducting an experiment at a lab table, sometimes reading a book, why not design the room to be functional? The teachers agreed. In the end, the room had a discourse center with five couches (donated by parents), science lab tables, study carrels from the library for "quiet work," computers, collaborative work tables, a *small-group mini-lesson* area, and individual desks.

Elementary school students are used to having a desk in which to store their belongings, but that would not be the case in this classroom. Instead, students received two personal-space structures. A set of cubbies were used for them to store their books. To personalize their cubbies, students designed thin strips of paper to decorate the left and top sides of each cubby. Additionally, the teachers marked off boxes on the cinderblock walls so that each student had a "My Best Work" area to post whatever work they wanted.

On the first day of school, the teachers met the students in the gymnasium and handed each of them a large puzzle piece. Their first order of business was to find the other three students whose puzzle pieces matched theirs. The completed puzzle gave them a direction in which to move from the doorway, for example, "walk northwest forty steps." (The "northwest" designation was used to reinforce cardinal directions.) They arrived at one of the functional areas of the classroom and then followed the directions there. For example, in the reading area they were asked to select a book from the shelf, identify the author, and make a prediction about the book from the cover. After about fifteen minutes, they were to move to the next area, again, using cardinal directions. At the cubby area, they decorated their cubbies. In the science area, they conducted a short experiment. At the *small-group mini-lesson* area, they met with one of the teachers to learn more about the class. At the couch area, they participated in a discussion with another one of the teachers. It took students three days to move through all the areas of the room and familiarize themselves with all of the structures of the *Learner-Active, Technology-Infused Classroom*. While this very structured movement through the classroom areas gave way to a more fluid, student-centered use of time and space, on the opening days of school, it provided a meaningful way for students to take charge of learning the various functional areas of the classroom as well as the structures and strategies that would support *student responsibility for learning*.

CONSIDER

In the *Learner-Active, Technology-Infused Classroom*, many of the decisions you make will be focused on the question, "Why?" The physical layout of the classroom is no exception. The dominant paradigm for classroom layout is to provide each student with a seat and desk or tabletop space, and then provide additional areas such as lab tables, reading corners, computer stations, meeting area, and so forth. The result is often a crowding of furniture in the room.

Instead, consider designing your class functionally so that when students enter the room, they go to the area that matches the function of the activity in which they will be engaged. In the *Learner-Active, Technology-Infused Classroom*, where students are scheduling their own time and learning activities are differentiated, using space functionally gives you the greatest number of options in the classroom. Of course, it begs the question: How do you offer a *benchmark lesson* to the entire class? As you design the space, think about what that particular learning situation might look like. If you have tables in the room, it may mean that more students sit at a table than usual in order to listen to your lesson. It may mean that students sit around the periphery of the room at lab tables or computer tables. It may mean students are sitting on a couch and listening. You need to make it work for you. I'm not suggesting that you should only have one available spot in the classroom for each student; but I am suggesting that you do not have a seat at a desk for each student in addition to many other work areas in the room.

This requires a paradigm shift. I've seen teachers set up rows of student desks and then place desktop computers around the periphery of the room. Students either all listened to the lecture or all worked on a computer. This wastes a valuable resource in the computers when students are all listening to a lesson; and it ends up failing to maximize the teacher's time when all students are on computers. Fewer computers could be used throughout the day or class period if students were working on different activities from their peers and if teachers used a variety of ways of teaching skills rather than reverting to whole-class, teacher-directed lessons.

I've also seen teachers focus so heavily on the concept of every student facing front to listen to a lesson, that they declined other furniture, such as round tables and couches, so as to preserve the desks facing the front of the room. My response to that is that you should design your classroom for what occurs in it ninety percent of the time, not ten percent. The amount of time you address the entire class should be minimal, so take the opportunity to design a rich and engaging physical environment for the more student-centered activities.

It may turn out that you have little control over your physical space. I have been in science labs where the tables were bolted to the floor. It may be that you share a classroom with other teachers and cannot make a lot of physical changes. If you are limited in the amount of control you have over physical space, read through this chapter to get a sense of the thinking behind the suggestions. You never know what change you may be able to effect over time. Remember that the three teachers in the "Big Room" managed to get their school district to take down a cinderblock wall.

CREATE

A great way to start is to take a piece of paper and draw out your current classroom or, if you don't yet have a classroom, how you expect to set up your classroom. Include all of the various areas, furniture, and structures. Then, on a separate piece of paper, for each area of the room, write about *why* you chose to set it up that way. After you complete this reflective exercise, you'll be in a better position to rethink the physical layout of your classroom. Think through each of the following sections and consider how you could arrange your room. Be open to possibilities, but don't commit to anything until you've finished reading through all of them.

Some physical space could be used to serve the purpose of two or more areas. As you read through each, focus on the purpose and then find the physical space to address the need.

Collaborative Work Space

Learning is often a collaborative effort. Outside of school, students naturally learn from one another. Brainstorming and higher-order thinking are typically enhanced through collaboration. Students need a place with a table top surface to write, draw, and work with their peers. This tends to be the largest amount of physical space allocated in the *Learner-Active, Technology-Infused Classroom*. You will probably want to provide enough collaborative space to accommodate approximately fifty to sixty percent of your students at one time.

Moving student desks together does not provide the best collaborative environment as students still have their own desks and clearly delineated personal space. Desks are often different heights and don't lend themselves well to creating a single work surface. Round tables that are forty-two inches in diameter are my choice. Students share the table top surface, no one has a specific, marked area, and the roundness and smallness foster a small-group environment. Although schools have a tendency to purchase forty-eight-inch-round tables, that extra six inches adds tremendously to the overall noise in the classroom. Smaller tables can be useful for conversations but not for having laptops, notebooks, and other materials in front of students. I've designed classrooms with, for example, four forty-two-inch-round tables and two thirty-six-inch-round tables. Rectangular and square tables tend to take up more space, and they do not engender a feeling of collaboration as well as a small, round table. Some teachers prefer the trapezoid tables that when paired create a hexagonal table. With these, however, the final table size tends to be very large and there's still a break down the middle, which I find does not foster collaboration as well as an unbroken, flat surface.

Individual Work Space

Students need to work alone to build individual content mastery, particularly when it comes to skill building. They can certainly engage in individual work at a round table, but sometimes they will want to be separated from their peers to work on their own. I advocate having two or three individual desks in the classroom for this purpose. This also allows a student who is a behavior problem or who cannot concentrate to move to an area apart from peers.

Teachers ask me about students who are diagnosed with attention-deficit disorder (ADD) or attention-deficit hyperactivity disorder (ADHD) and may not be able to concentrate with the amount of stimulation that is typical of collaborative and student-centered classrooms. My answer is always that students need to learn to accommodate for their learning difficulties, and what better place to learn this skill than in the classroom. The teachers in the "Big Room" borrowed a few study carrels from the media center. When students knew they needed to remove themselves to concentrate on their work, they moved to a study carrel.

The idea of "hoteling" has become popular in the corporate world. It speaks to the idea that not everyone is always in the building all of the time; so cubicles, desks, and offices should not lie vacant when they can be used by others. For example, if a company has 100 employees, but many of them are in sales or otherwise on the road such that no more than sixty are in the office at once, why should forty percent of the physical space always remain vacant? Some of your students' parents may be working in such a situation; and your students may face this when they enter the work world. In the case of "hoteling," workers sign up to reserve a particular office, cubicle, or desk. This also can apply to certain areas in the classroom.

In the elementary grades, I've seen teachers take large cardboard boxes (e.g., the type that are used to transport refrigerators and washers), cut off the tops and bottoms, and place them around a student desk to create a sense of being in a cubicle. Students then have nameplates with Velcro on the back that stick to the front of the cardboard cubicle. If a cubicle is empty, a student may choose to work there on independent work. I once saw a student move to a study carrel, pull out a picture of her family and a stuffed toy, set up her "office," and get to work. These items added a personal touch to the work environment.

Discourse Centers

Oral communication skills are important yet not always supported in the conventional approach to classrooms. Verbal acuity is one of the outcomes of learning in a *Learner-Active, Technology-Infused Classroom*, both through collaborative work and meaningful discussions.

Suppose students need to sit and have a discussion about a *problem-based task* or a book they are reading. A couch area can provide a wonderful discourse center, making students feel like they're at home engaging in a conversation in the living room. When the area is not used for discussions, students may use it to work collaboratively or independently. I was in one classroom where I sat down next to a young man on the couch who was surrounded on the couch and floor by graphic organizers. I asked him about his work and he explained the writing project in progress. Then he looked up at me and said, "Aren't you the one who said to get couches in the classroom?" I responded, "I am," at which point he patted the couch surface next to him and said, "Nice touch." A couple of couches can give a nice, homey feeling to a classroom.

You can also create a discourse center using a carpeted area and/or bean-bag chairs. In high schools, integrated chairs and desk surface units can be arranged in a circle to create a discourse center as well. Think about the best arrangement for you to provide your students with an area to have a discussion with you or among themselves.

Computer Areas

Nowadays, more schools are turning to laptops and one-to-one ratio of computing devices to students, so you may not need to allocate as much space to a computer area. In the "Big Room," each teacher originally had four computers in the classroom; so together, they had twelve. They designated eight of them for students to sign up for a forty-minute block. The remaining four were in a "Quick Lookup" area. Students could go to a computer to conduct a quick search for information, spending no more than five minutes at a computer. This way, there were always computers available to answer that spontaneous question or need for information.

Even if you are using laptop computers, you may want to have a desktop computer or two that offer special-purpose peripherals like a scanner, midi keyboard, or video camera. This could serve as a work area for multimedia production.

Resource and Folder Area

In an effort to encourage students to take greater responsibility for their own learning, you'll need a *resource area* from which students can retrieve the printed materials, such as *how-to sheets*, and small resources they may need for their work. Additionally, you will need a place where students will deposit their two-pocket *student work folders* at the end of the day or class period and pick them up when they return to class.

Often, teachers utilize a rectangular table, located in some area of the room, sometimes using tent cards to label materials or sections. Some teachers staple folders on a bulletin board so that students can retrieve papers from there. Others use storage boxes with file folders. Although it is more difficult to easily locate the desired material, storage boxes take up less room and can be stored away or moved if you share a classroom with other teachers. Storage boxes or crates also make a good receptacle for collecting student folders. In a 1:1 computing environment, the *resource area* becomes a Web-resident or networked folder for most materials.

Small-Group Mini-Lesson Area

You will need a space that will accommodate approximately six students attending a *small-group mini-lesson* with you. Keep the space condensed enough that students can hear you without you having to speak so loudly that the rest of the class can hear you. You'll want the ability to display information for the group. Some teachers create this area near a blackboard or whiteboard. Others use an easel pad on a tripod stand.

You want to be a part of the group, building *social capital*, so you would not want to sit behind your desk with students in front of you. Some teachers use kidney-shaped tables, others use round or rectangular tables, and still others use a set of individual chairs with an attached table surface. Given that students will be building skills, ensure that they will have a writing surface on which to work. Thus, having students sit on the floor around you is probably not the best arrangement for this area.

Meeting Area

You may decide to create a meeting area where your students can gather to meet with you for concept development or overall direction in approaching a unit of study. In primary classrooms, this is often a carpeted area in the center or a corner of the room. It allows the class to sit in a concentrated area to meet with the teacher. Primary teachers often have morning meetings in which they post a large letter to the students for the day. By reading this together, students learn about any announcements for the day while building reading skills and becoming familiar with letter format. In the upper grades, the meeting area might double as the discourse center. In the case of a couch area, it may involve having students pull over additional chairs, as you need to fit the entire class.

Limited Resource Area

I heard someone describing to me just recently how in her school, students use manipulatives to explore certain math concepts, but then, when the lesson was done, the manipulatives moved on to another class. If some students hadn't quite yet grasped the concept, they would have to continue their work without the manipulatives. This is not an uncommon occurrence in schools. The dominant paradigm for conventional teaching prescribes that all students have access to a particular resource at the same time. All students work with manipulatives; all students work on computers to construct a journal article; all students look at an onion skin under a microscope. This approach to resource utilization can prove to be costly and ineffective. Instead, consider having a smaller number of resources available in the classroom for a longer period of time. Five sets of manipulatives could remain in the classroom for the year, shared by students who sign up for particular timeslots. One or two microscopes could be used by students through the year rather than by everyone for one particular lesson.

A limited resource may be set up in its own physical area, such as in the case of a microscope, ant farm, sculpting wheel, listening center, and so forth. Other limited resources may be housed in containers and stored on a shelf, as in the case of math manipulatives, art supplies for a particular project, educational games, jump ropes, small percussion instruments, and so forth. In both cases, however, students will sign up for an available timeslot to make use of this limited resource. Decide what limited resources your students will need and where in your room you will allocate space for them.

Use the Walls

Consider how you will make meaningful and purposeful use of your classroom walls. Create a *quality work board* to offer inspiration for producing high-quality work. Designate a *help board* for students to sign up for your help when you are available. Provide areas for students to post their own work. Display various references around the room so that students gain valuable information at a glance. This might include a color wheel, regular polygons, the alphabet, a word wall, common words in a world language, parts of speech, the periodic chart, and more. If you share a room, consider a trifold presentation board that students can set up at the beginning of class and store away at the end of class.

Rather than thinking of your walls as something to decorate, consider how they can serve as a valuable resource for your students in the learning process. Creative use of the walls can add a lot of instructional space to the classroom.

How Big the Screen?

Shifting paradigms requires thoughtful reflection on the "why" of one's actions. The invention of the interactive whiteboard triggered a purchasing frenzy across schools. The interactive whiteboards were designated to be placed in the front of the classroom by the same administrators who were promoting a move from lecture-based instruction to student-centered instruction. This physical setup perpetuates the dominant paradigm of whole-class instruction with everyone looking at the screen in the front of the room. This phenomenon demonstrates how difficult it is to shift paradigms. These devices could be installed in a corner of the room for student *collaboration* and *small-group mini-lessons*.

I was working with a group of teachers who had been allocated a specified amount of money to purchase resources for their classrooms. They came to me to say that they wanted to purchase twenty-seven-inch televisions that could also serve as computer monitors. I asked them to think about their use in the classroom. One of the goals of the *Learner-Active, Technology-Infused Classroom* is to always use the talents of the teacher to the fullest. If the entire classroom is watching a DVD segment, the teacher is sitting idle, not sharing valuable expertise, talents, and knowledge with students. As we continued to discuss the *why* behind this, the teachers realized that they were falling into the trap of the conventional paradigm. Instead, they purchased smaller television/DVD combination units and designated them as limited-resource areas. If students were to watch a particular video segment, they would sign up to watch with a couple of peers and answer a set of prediscussion questions, to be later addressed with the entire class.

Any time you are inclined to set up an area of the classroom or purchase a resource that the entire class can use at the same time, stop and ask yourself why. You may find that as you apply the paradigm shifts of the *Learner-Active, Technology-Infused Classroom*, you arrive at a very different decision.

The Teacher's Desk

Consider how much teacher space is designated in the classroom. In some classrooms, the teacher has a desk, side table, and a couple of file cabinets all positioned across the front of the room, away from the board, thereby designating about five to seven feet of the front of the room for the teacher's use. In the *Learner-Active, Technology-Infused Classroom*, when students are in the room, teachers are never seated at their desks or working apart from students. Teachers spend their time facilitating learning and instructing. So all of that "teacher space" goes unused.

I've had teachers decide to remove their desk from the classroom to provide for more space, indicating that when students aren't in the room, they can use any table or desk to accomplish their work. All they need are some file cabinets and/or bookcases for their belongings, and those can fit in a corner of a room or against a wall. I've had teachers ask for smaller desks and/or push their desks against a side wall to open up more space in the room.

In one coteaching classroom, the teachers asked for two teachers' desks so that both teachers would be seen as being equally important. Within a short period of time, they both asked to have their desks removed, realizing they took up too much space.

Consider how much space is designated in your classroom for the teacher. Take time to rethink furniture choices and positions.

RECAP

The physical classroom space supports your philosophy of teaching and learning. As you design your *Learner-Active, Technology-Infused Classroom*, consider how you can rethink the use of physical space to create an environment that is aligned with your philosophy. This chapter outlined several areas for you to consider. Use these summary points as you reflect:

- ◆ Collaborative Work Space
- ◆ Individual Work Space
- ◆ Discourse Centers
- ◆ Computer Areas
- ◆ Resource and Folder Area
- ◆ Small-Group Mini-Lesson Area
- ◆ Meeting Area
- ◆ Limited Resource Area
- ◆ Use of the Walls as Instructional Resources
- ◆ The "Why?" of Your Decisions
- ◆ The Teacher's Desk

9

Ten Principles of the Learner-Active, Technology-Infused Classroom

The *Learner-Active, Technology-Infused Classroom* embodies ten principles. Throughout this book, you've explored all of these principles. Review the unit and classroom plan you're designing to see what structures and strategies you might want to add to foster these principles.

Higher-Order, Open-Ended Thinking

While it is true that one must master the lower levels of Bloom's Taxonomy before achieving the higher, attempting to build higher-order skills creates a *felt need* for the lower order. Deciding where to build an airport requires skills of map reading, graph reading, research, and more. Devising a plan for a bio dome on the moon requires concepts and skills related to ecosystems and living things.

Students will work tirelessly to solve a motivating problem.

What Higher-Order, Open-Ended Thinking Looks Like in the Classroom

- ◆ Rather than merely presenting back information that they learned, students seek out information while learning to solve open-ended problems.

- ◆ Teachers construct problems whose solutions reside in the "unknown," forcing students to grapple with content that drives them back to what is "known."

- Students are given carefully crafted higher-order problems to solve that drive them to learn lower-order skills.

- Teachers design instructional activities that provide students with a challenge level slightly higher than their ability level, continuing to build toward higher and higher levels of cognitive function.

- Teachers function as instructional facilitators, asking questions that cause students to think at the higher levels of Bloom's Taxonomy.

- Students participate in a wide range of strategic learning activities that foster content attainment and reach for synthesis and evaluation.

High Academic Standards

Students can accomplish amazing things when faced with high expectations and instructional supports—the two go hand-in-hand. Raising academic rigor will only result in more failure if students are not provided with the support to achieve at high levels. Teachers must overcome the tendency to teach to the level of the lowest-performing students and, instead, teach to a high level and help all students reach that level through differentiated opportunities to learn.

Teachers often design their *analytic rubrics* so that most students can meet the Practitioner column without too much effort and many can reach the Expert column. Take your *analytic rubric*, cutout the novice column, shift the remaining columns to the left, and write a new Expert column. This will ensure that you are presenting academic challenges to all students.

Look at your room decorations and make sure that you are posting materials to the bulletin boards that offer higher expectations and not content your students should already know. Post resources that students can glance at while working that support their success. This may sound obvious, but take a look at your classroom walls and ask yourself, "If students get stuck learning this skill or concept, what is posted on the wall that will help them?"

When facilitating, ask probing questions to prompt higher-order thinking. Share information that raises expectations. Challenge students with suggestions.

Finally, your word choice in the classroom can be used to achieve *high academic standards*. Use terms that are related to your field, even at the youngest levels. Choose your words carefully. Think about the number of times you use "do" during the course of a conversation and, instead, use "conduct," "complete," "accomplish," and the like. If you use a word that is new to your students, introduce the word and its meaning. For example, "I appreciate your veracity…your truthfulness." The student just learned a new word. Cognitively, at the point you say "veracity," the student will most likely wonder what the word means, creating a level of cognitive dissonance. By then hearing the definition, the student will most likely remember it.

What High Academic Standards Look Like in the Classroom

- The expert column of an *analytic rubric* pushes students to tackle extended content and greater higher-order thinking related to the content.

- The classroom walls are filled with resources to push student thinking.

- The teacher introduces vocabulary words, defining them in the sentence, while speaking.

- The teacher uses sophisticated sentence structure and grammar as modeling for students.

- When facilitating, the teacher asks questions that probe thinking, offers new information, and presents challenges.

Learning from a Felt Need

Years ago, I was teaching a high school computer science class in programming. It was a time when text-based, computerized adventure games were popular—before computer graphics! On the first day of class, I had my students play these computer games and write about their experiences. At the end of the period, I told them that during the semester, they were going to design original programs. First, they had to map out their ideas for their games; then they would begin to write the programs. When my students needed to display text on the screen, I taught them how by offering a *how-to sheet* or a *small-group mini-lesson*. When they needed to refer to the player by name, I likewise taught them how to store variables. When a few were ready to keep track of the items the player picked up during the game, I taught them to use arrays (multivariable structures.) I then established them as *peer tutors* as an option for their classmates. I carefully constructed the *problem-based task* so that students would need to use all of the concepts and skills in the curriculum. They learned through a *felt need*.

It can be easier just to present content to students; however, it is unlikely that they will remember it past the test, if that far. When students experience a *felt need* to learn, and they are then provided with just-in-time instruction, they retain that learning.

What Learning from a Felt Need Looks Like in the Classroom

♦ Students are presented with *problem-based tasks* at the start of a unit of study that drive the need to learn concepts and skills.

♦ Teachers ask students to read the *analytic rubric* at the start of a unit, identifying what they will need to learn in order to address the problem. From there, the teachers design instructional opportunities.

♦ Teachers offer *small-group mini-lessons* based on students' articulated needs.

♦ Students can explain why they are doing whatever activity they are doing and connect it to a greater instructional goal.

♦ Students access learning resources as they need them from a *resource area* and online sources.

♦ Students seek out additional resources in order to explore their own interests further.

Global Citizenship

In his book, *The World is Flat*, Thomas Friedman (2006) presents ten major events that have led to the increasing globalization of our society. Technology has played a significant role in leveling the playing field economically across the globe. In a flat world, someone using a product in the South America may be helped by someone in India. The distance between people around the world is greatly reduced by the ability to videoconference, e-mail, and send instant messages at a cost no different from talking to one's neighbor.

People are becoming increasingly aware of others around the world. Events in one part of the world affect the entire world economically, environmentally, and politically. We can no longer refer to ourselves as just citizens of our towns or countries: we are rapidly becoming world citizens.

The *Learner-Active, Technology-Infused Classroom* provides students with many opportunities for building their skills as *global citizens*. Make direct connections to other countries in your classroom activities. Students can engage in online activities with students in other parts of the world.

Build students' overall awareness of other countries. Students studying government structures can identify similar governments in countries around the world. Students can trace inventions to other countries; and they can look at today's manufacturing cycle in terms of other countries around the world.

Build students' cultural acceptance of others around the world. You can begin with your students' national heritage and explore cultural customs and beliefs that exist today in those countries. In their lifetimes, students may visit and/or work in other countries. Technology will allow them to work virtually with people from around the world.

Build students' higher-order skills of analyzing cause-and-effect relationships among countries. As your students work to solve problems, have them consider what impact, if any, their solutions will have on other parts of the world.

What Global Citizenship Looks Like in the Classroom

- ♦ Students gather information through the Internet on issues and events from around the world.

- ♦ Students engage in authentic learning units (*ALUs*) that require a knowledge of and consideration for countries around the world.

- ♦ Students follow news from around the world and relate it to their own studies.

- ♦ Students engage with outside experts and students around the world through technology, showing evidence of their understanding of cultural differences.

- ♦ Teachers provide learning opportunities for students to interact with members of the larger community in which they live.

- ♦ Students participate in service projects that have an impact on their schools, town, state, country, and the world.

Technology Infusion

The *Merriam-Webster* online dictionary definition of the word *integrate* is "to form, coordinate or blend into a functioning or unified whole"; the definition of the word *infuse* is "to cause to be permeated with something... that alters usually for the better." For far too long, the use of technology in the classroom has begun with the technology itself, assuming that if we take the goal of studying spreadsheets and the goal of studying immigration patterns, we can blend the two into one project with two goals. This is integration.

When technology permeates the classroom setting, students who are studying immigration naturally turn to the Internet to search for information, use spreadsheets to generate graphs, use videoconferencing to interview immigrants, use multimedia to present a position statement, and more. Technology is not the goal; immigration is. Technology is merely a ubiquitous partner in the learning process. This is the goal of technology infusion.

Computer technology should be seamlessly infused into the classroom curriculum, with perhaps key benchmarks at certain grade levels. Computers need to be nearly as readily available as pencils, and with smaller and less-expensive computing devices, this is a real possibility for the near-term future.

Learning how to use technology should be a "just-in-time" experience. Teaching students the A to Z of using a particular application fails to honor brain research and the need to build sense and meaning to maximize retention. As students use various applications, *how-to sheets* and video resources can provide them with specific skill instruction to meet their needs. It is not important to learn how to center a title if you are not using titles in your paper. At the point you need to learn to center a title, it is important that you know where to look to find the information. These days, much of that information can be found on the Internet.

Technology should be seamlessly infused into the learning environment with students accessing hardware and software as needed to pursue the greater goals of completing their *problem-based tasks*. When used effectively, technology becomes a powerful partner in the learning process, and particularly, for differentiating instruction.

What Technology Infusion Looks Like in the Classroom

- ◆ Students seek out technology when they need it, in the course of pursuing other learning goals.

- ◆ Technology is readily available all of the time in the classroom.

- ◆ Teachers use technology to deliver lessons, have students engage in learning situations, communicate with students and parents, gather and analyze student achievement data, and more.

- ◆ Technology is utilized to provide multiple means of representation (*Universal Design for Learning*) for students at various learning readiness levels.

Individual Learning Path

Clearly, there are not enough hours in a day to set up an *individual learning path* for every student and monitor each student's progress. This is why *individual learning path* and *student responsibility for learning* go hand-in-hand. If you provide students, even the youngest, with tools for assessing their own learning style preferences, and you offer various learning options, they will learn to make appropriate choices, with you providing guidance on those choices.

A middle school teacher had students begin the year by completing an online assessment of their learning styles, which provided a graph of their preferences. They then designed business cards to hand out to their teachers, so their teachers would get to know them. More importantly, the students themselves became aware of how some preferred listening to someone offer directions while others preferred seeing a written set of directions and diagram.

Some teachers use the "Learning Styles and Readiness Grid" (see Appendix I, page 184) as an option sheet from which students select activities, based on their preferences and abilities. It's not unusual for primary level teachers to offers students book selections with different levels of difficulty from which students choose, with the teacher's feedback.

Assessment should not be merely a tool of the teacher; students should self-assess to become aware of their cognitive strengths and weaknesses. As the teacher and student determine where the student needs to build greater skills, together they can lay out a plan for success. When students are treated as partners in their own instructional plan, they make many decisions independent of the teacher.

A fourth-grade math teacher and I developed structures to allow students to develop their own *individual learning paths*. She would give students a math pretest consisting of five questions from each key skill in the unit. Students then self-scored the tests and analyzed their results. If they answered all five questions on a skill correctly, they completed a challenge activity that presented them with a higher cognitive level problem using that skill. If they answered three to four questions correctly, they completed two to three activities that focused on practicing the skill. If they answered one or two questions on a skill correctly, they completed activities related to building the skill, including required computer activities, podcasts, *peer tutor* sessions, or *small-group mini-lessons*. If they did not answer any questions correctly, they began with introductory skill-building activities. This may sound like a lot of work—and it is up front—but consider how this approach allows students to follow an *individual learning path*. Once the pretests and activities are in place, the teacher is free to facilitate, advise, and offer targeted lessons. The following year, materials may need to be reviewed and modified, but with far less effort than the initial year. The initial outlay of effort on the part of the teacher to design structures to build an *individual learning path* pays off in higher student achievement, more meaningful interactions with students, and decreased effort in lesson design over the long-term.

What Individual Learning Path
Looks Like in the Classroom

♦ Teachers utilize assessment data to craft individual student plans to address the standards, suggesting specific activities or creating individualized expectations for students.

♦ Students follow personal activity lists that address their learning styles and cognitive levels.

♦ Students self-assess content mastery and skill level, sharing their analysis with the teacher to mutually agree upon a learning path.

♦ Teachers provide varied activities for building content and skill mastery such that students can engage in those that are most well-suited for them.

♦ Students make decisions about how they will learn a skill or build content mastery.

Student Responsibility for Learning

Consider two compelling reasons for building *student responsibility for learning*. First, it will make your work easier in that students will make informed decisions about how to master curricular goals. Second, students will not always have you around to guide them as they learn throughout their lives. Conventional wisdom places teachers in an authority role in which they tell students what to do, when to do it, and how to do it, with the belief that students would fail without that level of direction. In the *Learner-Active, Technology-Infused Classroom*, the emphasis is on building students' skills in self-assessment and decision making in the learning process such that they can truly become lifelong learners.

Children are inquisitive from birth. From the time they can talk, they start asking questions and they explore everything within their reach. The quest for learning is innate, and children learn a tremendous amount from their peers. A young skateboarder sees an interesting move and begins to put a plan into place to learn that move. It may include watching others in person, on television, and on videos posted on the Internet. It may include creating a practice course and making it increasingly harder. It may include endless hours of practice. Your students know how to take charge of their learning, but schools teach them early on simply to listen to the teachers and do as they are told, thus squelching this natural pursuit of learning.

If you asked me to teach you the parts of speech, I could sit down and describe each one and offer examples, but that would merely be telling you and expecting you to memorize, not fostering a learning environment. Alternatively, I could design a set of activities that would allow you to engage with sentences and explore the interrelationships that exist among the words, thus building in you a knowledge of the parts of speech that would last a lifetime. The former is easier; the latter requires great forethought and planning. However, in the case of the former, I will be presenting that lesson over and over again with student after student, year after year. In the case of the latter, I will design it once and empower a great number of students to take responsibility for learning, with only minor revisions across the years. The upfront investment required for designing the *Learner-Active, Technology-Infused Classroom*, which depends heavily on the principle of *student responsibility for learning*, will pay off considerably in student achievement and a greater sense of efficacy for you, the teacher.

What Student Responsibility for Learning Looks Like in the Classroom

- ♦ Students schedule their own time in the classroom based on the teacher's articulated expectations, choices of a diverse range of learning activities, and availability of a variety of resources.

- ♦ Students use *analytic rubrics*, checklists, and other structures to self-assess and set goals, with the guidance of the teacher.

- ♦ Students reflect on their progress and practices and make adjustments to become more effective and productive learners.

Connected Learning

Students are motivated by real-world events, fueled by accessibility via the Internet. Brain research demonstrates that it is important to connect learning to students' lives; the reality-based shift in society provides additional evidence of the importance of *connected learning*.

Problem-based tasks provide the real-world authenticity for learning; the next step is to make deliberate connections to students' lives. Science teachers launch into the study of genetics by having students analyze their own genetic traits. Health teachers have students study their own nutrition. In designing *problem-based tasks*, consider the activities or requirements that could be used to connect the learning to students' lives.

Connected learning also means connecting learning across the disciplines. Given the departmentalized nature of school, students do not always see how one subject's skills and concepts relate to the next.

What Connected Learning Looks Like in the Classroom

♦ Students engage in *problem-based tasks* based on real-world scenarios.

♦ Students engage in activities that ask students to reflect on the content based on their own lives and experiences.

♦ Students articulate how content from other subject areas helped them in completing the *problem-based task*.

♦ Teachers present connections to other subject areas in their *benchmark lessons, small-group mini-lessons*, and other instructional materials.

♦ Teachers use the Expert column of *analytic rubrics* to encourage students to explore further related content of interest.

Collaboration

Cooperative learning describes a group working together and typically dividing up tasks to complete a particular assignment. The word *cooperate* intimates "putting up with one another" for the common good. For example, if the class wants to get to lunch on time, everyone should cooperate and get on line and be quiet. *Collaborate*, on the other hand, intimates that some new knowledge is going to be developed based on the "two-heads-are-better-than-one" principle. *Collaboration* results in an end product that is enhanced by the input of more than one person; thus, collaborative activities are open-ended and focused on higher-order thinking.

Problem-based tasks offer students rich opportunities to collaborate. Devising a plan to convince an author to write a book about your town, deciding on where to build an airport, developing ideas for cleaning up a local river, developing a campaign to engage young people today in Shakespeare's work, proposing a plan and budget for a class trip, writing an original song to promote school unity, and the like are all powerful venues for *collaboration*.

Consequently, it is important to carefully structure collaborative work. Students should work together to brainstorm, critique ideas, share relevant information, develop questions, and evaluate their work. They should work independently to research topics, build content mastery, and develop ideas to bring to the larger group. As you design your activity lists, be sure to build in a meaningful distinction between individual work and group work.

It can be useful to have students develop a set of "team norms" of expected rules of engagement, such as: one person speaks at a time, all members are encouraged to participate, and avoid monopolizing the conversation. Additionally, students need to be able to handle "roadblocks" that veer the discussion off topic. Construct a "roadblock management chart" by dividing a piece of paper into four quadrants. Label them:

◆ Off topic—save for a later discussion.

◆ We need more information that is not available right now—save until information is available.

◆ We do not have the authority to make this decision.

◆ We need other people to make this decision.

When students find themselves stuck in an unresolved conversation, they should stop and write down the current discussion points in one of the four quadrants. This allows them to capture the information and frees them to move on.

Students may also need collaborative brainstorming tools, such as Edward de Bono's "six hats" (1996) or "PMI" (1992). The six hats method has the students look at a problem or proposed solution from six perspectives. The yellow hat is optimistic, black hat is skeptical, red hat expresses emotion, green hat is creative, blue hat is into the organization of the process, and white hat focuses on objective facts. This method allows you to honor all perspectives, such as: "Put on your yellow hat for a minute and tell me what is great about this idea. Put on your black hat and tell me what could go wrong or why it won't work. Put on your green hat to see if you can come up with another idea."

PMI stands for Plus, Minus, and Interesting facts or questions. Students use a three-column sheet to analyze a possible solution or idea. In a short, designated amount of time, they write down two positive points, two negative points, and then two, related, interesting ideas or questions. Following personal reflection, each group member has an opportunity to share and be heard. Students in the group begin to see emerging trends and innovative ideas.

Both of these tools, and others, help students build their skills in critical thinking and problem-solving, which are important skills for collaboration. Consider introducing a new tool every couple of weeks to build your students' repertoire of collaborative work tools.

You'll want to establish a process for handling conflicts among team members as well. The first step should be to have the students sit down and talk about their differences to see if they can work it out. If that doesn't work, you might suggest the use of a peer mediator. Next, you might have the students sit down with you. Avoid allowing students to complain about one another to you without the other present. They are in a learning mode, so you do need to ensure that the collaborative relationships are productive and enhancing each student's individual progress. In your facilitation, you will get a sense if one student is not working to the effort of the rest of the team, if one student is being too bossy, and so forth. It is clearly better for you to assess the ability of the group members to work well collaboratively than it is for them to approach you and complain about one another. Ultimately, you want them to take responsibility for building collaborative relationships.

What Collaboration Looks Like in the Classroom

- Two to four students meet with a specific goal that is part of a greater problem-solving effort. For example, when deciding where to build the next airport, an early group effort would be to brainstorm everything the students need to know to begin to make a decision.

- Students are challenged, in groups, to solve open-ended problems requiring them to apply curricular content, through which they build mastery in that content.

- Students use various structures to ensure that all students have the opportunity to participate and that all group interactions are positive.

- Students take individual responsibility to contribute expertise and information to the group.

- Students take the responsibility for each member of the group being successful in both content mastery and group interactions.

- Students use Internet-based tools to work collaboratively both inside and outside the classroom.

- Students use Internet-based tools to work collaboratively with students in other classrooms and geographically distant locations.

High Social Capital

The term *social capital* dates as far back as 1916 (Hanifan) to an article on rural schooling pointing out that social networks bring a benefit to their members. A family is a social network as is a local community, work community, and, these days, online social communities. In more recent years, James Coleman (1988) popularized the term, suggesting that social networks, specifically local communities, had a direct correlation to the production of its members and the achievement of students in schools.

High social capital can be described as the relationships that are forged in a community between its adults and its young people. In communities that are characterized by *high social capital*, parents often know the names of other children in the neighborhood; they'll offer children they know a ride; they'll cheer for children at sporting events and congratulate individuals on their successes; they'll call one another to share what they saw, particularly if anything they see is suspicious. Children who grow up in communities with *high social capital* tend to do well in school. In communities that are characterized by low social capital, children move through the neighborhood seemingly unnoticed; often no one at home asks about them or their schooling; sometimes children are left home alone for long periods of time without anyone checking in on them; parents in the community do not necessarily know the other children nor engage with them. Children who grow up in communities with low social capital tend to struggle in school. Furthermore, children from communities with low social capital who attend private or parochial schools that foster *high social capital* tend to improve their academic performance.

Strong, caring relationships between adults and children contribute to improved student performance. These relationships are a characteristic of the *Learner-Active, Technology-Infused Classroom*. In conventional schooling, where teachers spent much of their time in the front of the room dispensing information, there are few opportunities to build relationships between adults and children. A student might enjoy a positive comment on a paper from a teacher, or the teacher might ask the student to linger after school to talk about accomplishments, and occasionally a teacher would be seen at a school event engaging in conversation with a student.

In the *Learner-Active, Technology-Infused Classroom*, teachers build strong relationships with students throughout the day. They increase social capital through the venue of the *small-group mini-lessons* where they are sitting with and talking to a small number of students, sharing information, asking questions, and encouraging students to succeed. Teachers have numerous one-on-one conversations with students throughout the course of the day. As teachers move throughout the classroom, the "never hover" rule causes teachers to pull up a chair and sit with students face to face, engaging in productive and motivating conversations about content.

In classrooms with more than one adult, such as the coteaching classroom, and in classrooms that regularly involve parents and community members, students enjoy considerable interaction with adults who care about them. This builds *high social capital*, which yields results in increased student achievement.

What High Social Capital Looks Like in the Classroom

♦ Teachers spend class time largely sitting with students discussing their work, goals, and accomplishments.

♦ Multiple adults work in the classroom with students, thus providing greater adult–student interaction.

- Teachers design *problem-based tasks* and instructional activities that require students to engage with their parents, family members, and other adults in their lives.

- Parents and community members are regular participants in the learning process, either in person or through virtual connections.

- Teachers develop online or print newsletters for the community that celebrate the successes of the students.

RECAP

Consider your classroom, the unit you are designing, and the overall activities, structures, and strategies that take place in your classroom. Continually reflect on how you can foster these ten principles in your classroom:

- Higher-Order, Open-Ended Problem Solving
- High Academic Standards
- Learning from a Felt Need
- Global Citizenship
- Technology Infusion
- Individual Learning Path
- Student Responsibility for Learning
- Connected Learning
- Collaboration
- High Social Capital

Appendices

The following appendices can also be found online at www.eyeoneduc-
tion.com and www.ideportal.com.

Appendix A
Airport Problem

People rely on airplanes daily to take them on important business trips or to their favorite vacation spots. However, as people travel more regularly, lines and waiting times at airports have begun to lengthen. Another airport in your state, depending on the location, could provide greater accessibility to air travel.

You are going to decide where an international airport should be built in your state. Make your recommendations based on facts and logical reasoning. Develop a persuasive argument in the form of a report, multimedia presentation, or video. Whichever you choose, create visuals to share information about the state and your decision, including a map of the suggested area.

	Novice	Apprentice	Practitioner	Expert
Location	makes statements to support location in 1 or more of the following areas: ♦ topography ♦ population centers ♦ accessibility by roadways or other transportation	offers facts to support location in 2 or more of the following areas: ♦ topography ♦ population centers ♦ accessibility by roadways or other transportation	offers facts to support location regarding: ♦ topography ♦ population centers ♦ accessibility by roadways or other transportation ♦ environmental factors	all of *Practitioner* plus anticipates and responds to arguments against location in one or more areas listed under *Practitioner*
Benefits of Location	identifies benefits	at least 4 benefits related to at least 2 different issues	at least 4 benefits related to 4 different issues	all of *Practitioner* plus includes short-term and long-term benefits

		Novice	Apprentice	Practitioner	Expert
Potential Negative Effects of Location		identifies at least 1 potential negative effect	2 or more potential negative effects	at least 4 potential negative effects and which groups might be opposed to the airport because of each	all of *Practitioner* plus weighs the pros and cons with evidence to support the location
Map of Proposed Airport Location		map includes: ♦ clearly marked location ♦ title ♦ compass rose ♦ cities ♦ landforms	map is drawn to scale and includes: ♦ clearly marked location ♦ title ♦ compass rose ♦ counties ♦ cities	all of *Apprentice* plus map is of a 50-mile radius of the location and includes relevant landforms, such as bay, desert, gulf, island, isthmus, lake, mesa, ocean, mountain, strait, peninsula, plateau, river, valley	all of *Practitioner* plus: ♦ latitude and longitude ♦ elevation of airport location and surrounding areas
Visuals	Choices	includes at least one chart or graph of related information	includes at least one chart and one graph that support recommendation	includes supportive charts and graphs and those that counter anticipated protests; all sources of data are cited	includes explanation of process for deciding which charts and graphs to include
	Quality	2 of 4 criteria under *Practitioner*	3 of 4 criteria under *Practitioner*	♦ neatly constructed ♦ titled ♦ labeled ♦ colored to make the data easier to understand	all of *Practitioner* plus at least one computer-generated graph that includes "what-if" analysis features

Appendix B
Radioactive
Waste Smorgasbord

Radioactive waste is dangerous, even deadly, to humans, but did you know that there are some single-celled life forms that actually consume it? Strange but true! Scientists have identified several species of bacteria that breathe uranium like we breathe oxygen. Some researchers believe we could use these bacteria to clean up radioactive pollution in water. Others think that there might be some serious consequences that we need to consider before we use a living being to clean up our toxic waste. As a budding micro-biological researcher, your task is to use the scientific method and think like a scientist. You will evaluate the data on these bacteria and decide how one or a combination of them would work effectively as microscopic radioactive pollution eaters. Then you must choose how to most effectively present your findings. Should it be an oral presentation? A scientific paper? A poster? A website? Your work will help make our world a little cleaner and safer!

Content Mastery Rubric

Criteria must be present in your log and/or your final product.

	Novice	Apprentice	Practitioner	Expert
Bacteria structure	beginning stages of diagram of bacteria cell structure	◆ diagram of bacteria cell structure ◆ images and description of how bacteria reproduce	◆ accurately labeled diagram of bacteria cell structure ◆ images and detailed description of how bacteria reproduce	*all of Practitioner plus* includes diagrams of 3 "uranium-eating" bacteria
Knowledge of "uranium-eating" bacteria	identifies 3 "uranium-eating" bacteria	identifies 3 "uranium-eating" bacteria and; includes detailed explanation of metabolism respiration for at least one	identifies 3 "uranium-eating" bacteria and, for each, includes detailed explanation of: ◆ metabolism ◆ respiration	*all of Practitioner plus* includes differences in habitat and oxygen tolerance

	Novice	Apprentice	Practitioner	Expert
Bacteria in the human body	identifies at least 1 bacteria that is found in the human body	identifies at least 1 bacteria that has a negative effect on the human body and 1 that has a positive effect	identifies at least 3 different incidences of bacteria in the human body (representing both positive and negative effects) and explains their role	*all of Practitioner plus* includes comments on the effects of eliminating each of these
Bacteria in the environment	identifies at least one bacteria that is found in the environment	identifies at least 1 bacteria that has a negative effect on the environment and 1 that has a positive effect	identifies at least 3 different incidences of bacteria in the environment (representing both positive and negative effects) and explains their role	*all of Practitioner plus* includes comments on the effects of eliminating each of these
Bacteria and uranium	identifies 3 different bacteria that interact with uranium to eliminate radioactive waste	explains how the 3 different bacteria interact with uranium to eliminate radioactive waste	details how 3 different bacteria interact with uranium to eliminate radioactive waste, including a description and cause-and-effect or process diagrams	*all of Practitioner plus* details conditions (i.e., oxygen and radioactivity levels) before, during, and after the time the bacteria are present

(Appendix B continues on next page.)

Laborasphere Process Rubric

	Novice	Apprentice	Practitioner	Expert
Log: Inquiry	keeps a log of information on the topic	keeps a log of information on the topic that includes personal knowledge, questions, knowledge learned, and/or experiments	◆ lists personal knowledge ◆ generates questions that relate to the task statement ◆ identifies experiments ◆ conducts experiments with precision; accurately records data ◆ keeps legible, meaningful notes with citations	*all of Practitioner* plus includes meaningful charts, graphs, drawings, and other visual aids
Log: Synergy	decides upon a specific problem solution to pursue	identifies the pieces of data that triggered the problem solution	identifies the pieces of data that triggered the problem solution; writes paragraph explaining the moment of synergy	*all of Practitioner* plus includes graphic of various pieces of information and the cause-and-effect relationship among the pieces
Log: Innovation	describes problem solution with evidence that solution will work	includes: ◆ evidence that solution will work ◆ implementation plan ◆ plausibility	includes: ◆ evidence that solution will work ◆ implementation plan ◆ plausibility on several levels ◆ possible unintended consequences	*all of Practitioner* plus maps out possible future cause-and-effect relationships (both positive and negative) well beyond the current time
Sources	at least 3 sources cited	at least 4 varied sources cited	at least 6 varied sources cited, including one scientific paper	*all of Practitioner* plus transcript or video from a personal interview with an expert

	Novice	Apprentice	Practitioner	Expert
Rigor	hypothesis generated from data	clearly stated hypothesis generated from data and supported through the scientific process	clearly stated hypothesis generated from data and supported through a well-documented scientific process	*all of Practitioner* plus multiple sources (including experiments) supporting the same data
Analysis	hypothesis discussed with data to prove it	two potential hypotheses discussed with data being used to disprove one	three or more potential hypotheses discussed with data being used to disprove all but one	*all of Practitioner* plus includes a flowchart of "if, then" statements analyzing the strength of the hypothesis
Reporting	includes background, experiments, and a conclusions section	♦ includes background, experiments, and a conclusions section ♦ presents data and conclusions drawn ♦ no more than 2 grammar, spelling, or punctuation errors	♦ includes background, experiments, and a conclusions section ♦ clear relationship between data presented and conclusions drawn ♦ no grammar, spelling, or punctuation errors	*all of Practitioner* plus includes at least three media elements (e.g., text, visuals, audio, video)

Appendix C
Ski Indoors!

Skiing is a popular sport, but avid skiers are constrained by the seasons, weather conditions, and time of day. Indoor ski slopes are gaining in popularity as they allow for the control of many of these constraints and could provide year-round fun. Still, the most interesting indoor ski slopes are probably yet to be designed. Try your hand at it! You are going to explore various existing indoor ski slopes and then develop a plan for an indoor ski center of your own. You'll need a healthy background knowledge of coordinate planes, slopes, lines, and graphing linear equations (those equations that produce straight lines). Your task is to graph the mathematical slope of various existing indoor ski slopes and design three unique ski slopes for varying abilities. Your ski slopes should be drawn carefully on graph paper and include the linear equations for the straight segments.

	Novice	Apprentice	Practitioner	Expert
Exist-ing ski slope explora-tion	♦ graphs at least 2 existing in-door ski slopes ♦ describes, by showing the slope of each section, at least 2 exist-ing indoor ski slopes	♦ graphs at least 5 existing in-door ski slopes ♦ describes, by showing the slope of each section, at least 5 exist-ing indoor ski slopes	♦ graphs at least 5 exist-ing indoor ski slopes, show-ing measure-ments from research ♦ describes, using a series of linear equa-tions, at least 5 existing in-door ski slopes	all of *Practitioner* plus compares and contrasts the 5 slopes using quantified slope, and discusses change in slope between sections
Unique ski slope design	designs at least 1 ski slope, each with at least 3 straight segments	designs at least 1 ski slope, each with: ♦ at least 3 straight seg-ments of vary-ing slopes ♦ proportions similar to exist-ing slopes	designs 3 differ-ent ski slopes, each with: ♦ at least 3 straight seg-ments ♦ proportions similar to exist-ing ski slopes ♦ slopes of straight seg-ments include slopes of >2 and <1	designs 3 differ-ent realistic ski slopes with a combined total of at least 20 straight seg-ments of varying slopes
Math-ematical descrip-tion	describes each straight segment including ♦ linear equation ♦ slope	describes each straight segment including ♦ linear equation ♦ slope ♦ *y*-intercept ♦ coordinates for 1 point on the segment	describes each straight segment including ♦ linear equation ♦ slope ♦ *y*-intercept ♦ coordinates for 3 points on the segment	all of *Practitioner* plus uses non-linear equations to describe the curved segments
Vocabu-lary	in descriptions appropriately uses terms: line, rise, and run	in descriptions appropriately uses terms: line, rise, run, slope, and, points	in descriptions appropriately uses terms: line, rise, run, slope, linear equation, points, and *y*-intercept	all of *Prac-titioner* plus uses additional related terms, e.g., tangent and derivative

(Appendix C continues on next page.)

Scaffold for Learning: Sampling of Activities

How-To Videos/Podcasts
- Creating a T-chart
- Graphing a linear equation

Interactive Web Sites
- Plotting points
- Exploring linear equations

Technology Uses
- Designing your Ski Slope in *Geometer Sketchpad*
- Developing T-charts in *Excel*

Peer Tutoring
- Plotting points
- Creating a T-chart
- Graphing a linear equation

Learning Centers
- Reading and Drawing Blueprints
- Linear Equations in Science

A Scaffold for Learning

Group Tasks
- "Mapping the neighborhood"
- Rise and Run
- "Navigating the Big Apple"
- "Investigating Skate Ramps" Finding the Y-intercept
- "How much did _____ cost?"

How-To Sheets
- Calculating the Pythagorean theorem
- Calculating slope
- Graphing a linear equation
- Graphing a point

Individual Tasks
- Finding Equations of Line segments
- Designing your Ski Slope using Graph paper

Homework
- Mapping your room
- Finding slopes around you
- Graphing linear equations practice

Benchmark Lessons
- Patterns of Change
- Describing lines with Math
- Math in Architecture
- Relationships among numbers

Small-Group Mini-Lessons
- Pythagorean theorem
- Graphing a linear equation
- Calculating slope
- Describing curves mathematically

Ski Indoors Facilitation Grid

	Finding Points	Reading Tables	Drawing Graphs	Writing Equations	Plotting Points	Finding the Rise	Finding the Run	Calculating Slope	Finding the y-Intercept	Writing Linear Equations from a Line	Writing Linear Equations from 2 Points

Appendix D
Declaring Independence

In the late eighteenth century, America struggled for its freedom from colonial rule and eventually produced the *Declaration of Independence*. Yet, according to the United Nations, a number of nations are *still* under colonial rule! In 1960, hoping to speed the progress of decolonization, the United Nations adopted the *Declaration on the Granting of Independence to Colonial Countries and Peoples*. This document declares that colonial rule should be brought to a speedy and unconditional end.

How will each nation that is currently under colonial rule declare its independence? You are to select a nation, research a little about its situation, and offer a set of recommendations for how it might work to declare its independence. To accomplish this, you are going to research the American Revolution for similarities, differences, and insights, paying particular attention to the United States' *Declaration of Independence* (*DoI*).

	Novice	Apprentice	Practitioner	Expert
Founding Principles of the *DoI*	♦ identifies 6 founding principles	♦ identifies 6 founding principles ♦ identifies what in history led to their inclusion in the *DoI*	♦ identifies 6 founding principles and what led to their inclusion in the *DoI* ♦ identifies how each principle is represented in present-day America	*all of Practitioner plus* relates each principle to the current situation in the colonial nation
Historical Perspective on the *DoI*	identifies at least 3 issues that served as catalysts for the fight for independence	identifies at least 3 issues that served as catalysts for the fight for independence and the areas of the with specific language in the *DoI* that addresses each	develops timeline of at least 3 catalyst issues that led to the decision for independence with specific language in the *DoI* that addresses each and the resolution of the issue in post-colonial times	*all of Practitioner plus*, for each issue, offers the British perspective on the issues
Evaluation of *DoI*	♦ 3 ways in which the *DoI* has been successful, citing specific examples	♦ 3 ways in which the *DoI* has been successful, citing specific examples ♦ 1–2 specific suggestions for improvement, given today's society	♦ at least 3 ways in which the *DoI* has been successful, citing specific examples ♦ at least 3 points of contention that have caused problems over the years ♦ 3 specific suggestions for improvement	*all of Practitioner plus* secondary effects that the recommended improvements would have in our culture

(Appendix D continues on next page.)

	Novice	Apprentice	Practitioner	Expert
Recommendations for Granting Independence	based on America's model for independence, makes 3 recommendations for the decolonization of the chosen country	based on America's model for independence, makes 4 recommendations, including the logic behind each recommendation	based on America's model for independence makes 5 recommendations, outlining specific parallels between the chosen country's and the United States' history	*all of Practitioner plus* cause-and-effect U.S. history timelines related to recommendations with predictions for future success of the chosen country's political, economic and social health
Delivery of Recommendations	Includes: ♦ statement of need for the chosen country to decolonize ♦ recommendations with support	Includes: ♦ statement of need for the chosen country to decolonize ♦ organized approach to information presentation ♦ some information outlined in the above four rows ♦ use of visuals	Includes: ♦ statement of need for the chosen country to decolonize ♦ organized approach to information presentation ♦ all information as outlined in the above 4 rows ♦ appropriate and varied persuasive writing techniques ♦ use of visuals to strengthen the case	*all of Practitioner* plus separate, personal statement of the process used to arrive at the recommendations

Declaring Independence Facilitation Questions

COMPREHENSION: Ask questions that ensure students understand content and skills needed to solve the problem.	◆ What is a colony? ◆ What does it mean to be independent? ◆ What does it mean to declare something? ◆ What is the purpose of the *Declaration of Independence*? ◆ What are the 16 nations currently under colonial rule? ◆ What resources will you use to assist you in conducting research on the decolonized nations? ◆ How do you evaluate something?
APPLICATION: Ask questions that ensure the ability of students to apply learning to new situations.	◆ What are the founding principles of the Declaration of Independence? ◆ What does decolonization mean? ◆ Why would a nation want to declare its independence? ◆ How would a nation declare its independence? ◆ What questions should you and your group members ask about the *Declaration of Independence* as it pertains to the 16 nations?
CONNECTION: Ask questions that ensure the ability of students to apply learning to their lives.	◆ What educational, human rights, political, and/or socioeconomic factors influence the current governing of these nations? ◆ What are the benefits of each of the 6 principles in present-day society? ◆ Cite 3 specific examples in which the Declaration of Independence has been a success? ◆ What are the various roles that each of your group members can assume as you conduct your research?

(Appendix D continues on next page.)

SYNTHESIS: Ask questions that encourage students to create new information from existing data.	♦ In critiquing the *Declaration of Independence*, what 5 recommendations would you suggest for the decolonization of your nation based on your research? ♦ Why should the nation declare its independence? ♦ What documents exist to aid the nation in declaring its independence? ♦ What are the implications of a nation declaring its independence? ♦ How if any, are the 6 principles represented in any of the 16 nations that are still under colonial rule? ♦ What factors have prevented these nations from declaring their independence? ♦ Are there any current trends in society that may have bearing on the nation's ability to declare independence?
METACOGNITION: Ask questions which prompt students to think about their own thinking process.	♦ What factors influenced your group's decision in make the recommendations for improvements to the *Declaration of Independence*? ♦ In reflecting on your groups assignment, is there anything that you would have done differently to assist you in creating your report? ♦ What conclusions arose while analyzing your group's report?

Declaring Independence Facilitation Grid

Makes connections between US de-colonization and modern colonization							
Explains reasons to choose to decolo-nize							
Describes benefits to colonialism							
Identifies countries currently under colonial rule							
Gives specific examples of liberties they still have							
Gives modern-day examples of the founding principles							
Describes the founding principles of the Declaration of Independence							
Identifies educational reasons the colonies wanted independence							
Identifies political reasons the colo-nies wanted independence							
Identifies socioeconomic reasons the colonies wanted independence							

(Appendix D continues on next page.)

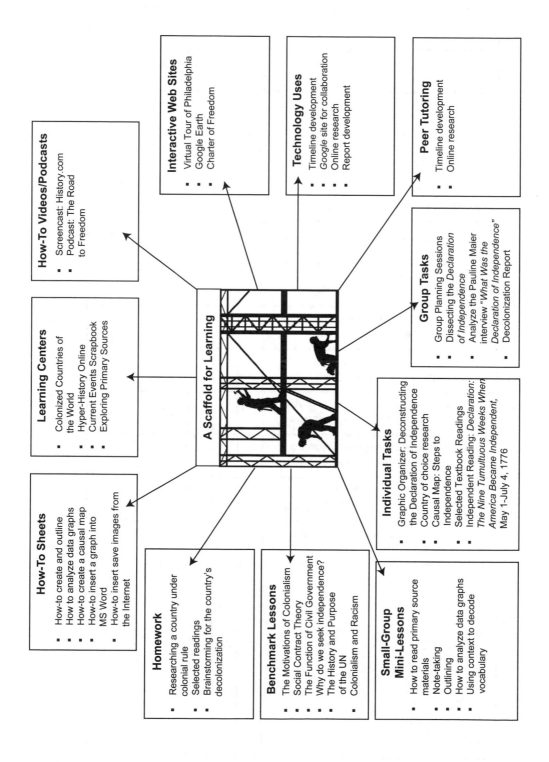

How-To Videos/Podcasts
- Screencast: History.com
- Podcast: The Road to Freedom

Interactive Web Sites
- Virtual Tour of Philadelphia
- Google Earth
- Charter of Freedom

Technology Uses
- Timeline development
- Google site for collaboration
- Online research
- Report development

Peer Tutoring
- Timeline development
- Online research

Learning Centers
- Colonized Countries of the World
- Hyper-History Online
- Current Events Scrapbook
- Exploring Primary Sources

A Scaffold for Learning

Group Tasks
- Group Planning Sessions
- Dissecting the *Declaration of Independence*
- Analyze the Pauline Maier interview "What Was the *Declaration of Independence*"
- Decolonization Report

How-To Sheets
- How-to create and outline
- How to analyze data graphs
- How-to create a causal map
- How-to insert a graph into MS Word
- How-to insert save images from the Internet

Individual Tasks
- Graphic Organizer: Deconstructing the Declaration of Independence
- Country of choice research
- Causal Map: Steps to Independence
- Selected Textbook Readings
- Independent Reading: *Declaration: The Nine Tumultuous Weeks When America Became Independent, May 1–July 4, 1776*

Homework
- Researching a country under colonial rule
- Selected readings
- Brainstorming for the country's decolonization

Benchmark Lessons
- The Motivations of Colonialism
- Social Contract Theory
- The Function of Civil Government
- Why do we seek independence?
- The History and Purpose of the UN
- Colonialism and Racism

Small-Group Mini-Lessons
- How to read primary source materials
- Note-taking
- Outlining
- How to analyze data graphs
- Using context to decode vocabulary

Appendix E
Author's Choice

You probably have some favorite fiction books that you have read. You may even have a favorite author whose books you like. When authors write a book, they usually start with a storyboard, that is, a plan for the book. They have to consider where they want the story to take place (the setting), who will be in the story (the characters), and what will happen in the story to make it interesting to the reader (the plot). All of this is up to the imagination of the author.

Suppose you wanted your favorite author to write a book set in your town? You would have to convince the author that your town is perfect for a new book. That would mean you would have to know a lot about the books your author has already written so that you could make connections and build a persuasive argument.

You are going to do just that! You are going to write a letter to your favorite author to make the case for writing a book set in your town. To do that, you are first going to have to read several of the author's books and consider the story elements in each so that you can use this information to make your case.

	Novice	Practitioner	Expert
Book Review	◆ reads 2 books by the same author ◆ writes opinion	◆ reads 3 books by the same author ◆ writes opinion that includes specific examples from story	all of *Practitioner* plus includes comparisons with other books
Graphic Organizer	identifies the following from each book: ◆ main characters ◆ setting ◆ plot	all of *Novice* plus identifies how your town is similar to or different from the setting	all of *Practitioner* plus includes ideas for how the author's characters and plot fit the town

(Appendix E continues on next page.)

	Novice	Practitioner	Expert
Letter Format	◆ greeting ◆ body ◆ signature	◆ date ◆ greeting ◆ body ◆ closing ◆ signature	all of *Practitioner* plus includes proper spaces and margins
Letter Content	◆ organized with clear beginning, middle and end ◆ provides 1–2 reasons for choosing town	◆ organized with clear beginning, middle and end ◆ provides 2–3 reasons for choosing town ◆ makes connections to the author's work	all of *Practitioner* plus explains how author can incorporate town into the new book
Capitalization	capitalizes: ◆ first word of sentence ◆ days and months	capitalizes: ◆ first word of sentence ◆ days and months ◆ proper nouns ◆ book titles	all of *Practitioner* plus does not capitalize prepositions in titles
Punctuation	uses correct punctuation at the end of sentences	◆ uses correct punctuation at the end of sentences ◆ uses quotation marks ◆ uses commas in dialogue	all of *Practitioner* plus uses commas to divide ideas in a complex sentence

Scaffold for Learning: Author's Choice

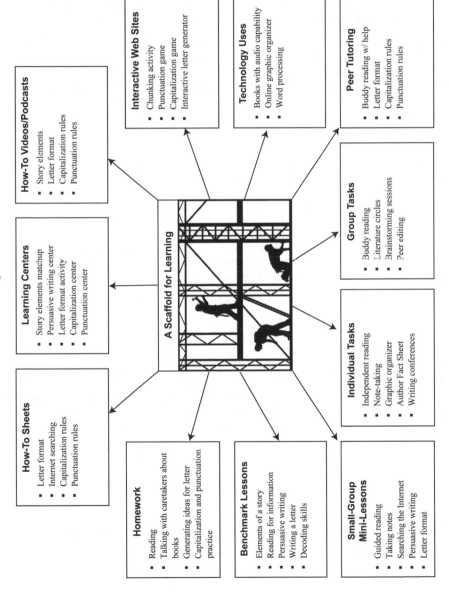

How-To Sheets
- Letter format
- Internet searching
- Capitalization rules
- Punctuation rules

Learning Centers
- Story elements matchup
- Persuasive writing center
- Letter format activity
- Capitalization center
- Punctuation center

How-To Videos/Podcasts
- Story elements
- Letter format
- Capitalization rules
- Punctuation rules

Interactive Web Sites
- Chunking activity
- Punctuation game
- Capitalization game
- Interactive letter generator

A Scaffold for Learning

Technology Uses
- Books with audio capability
- Online graphic organizer
- Word processing

Peer Tutoring
- Buddy reading w/ help
- Letter format
- Capitalization rules
- Punctuation rules

Group Tasks
- Buddy reading
- Literature circles
- Brainstorming sessions
- Peer editing

Individual Tasks
- Independent reading
- Note-taking
- Graphic organizer
- Author Fact Sheet
- Writing conferences

Homework
- Reading
- Talking with caretakers about books
- Generating ideas for letter
- Capitalization and punctuation practice

Benchmark Lessons
- Elements of a story
- Reading for information
- Persuasive writing
- Writing a letter
- Decoding skills

Small-Group Mini-Lessons
- Guided reading
- Taking notes
- Searching the Internet
- Persuasive writing
- Letter format

(Appendix E continues on next page.)

Differentiation Grid Skill: Decoding Skills—Chunking

	DISTAL ZONE	PROXIMAL ZONE	CURRENT KNOWLEDGE
	A student who will be challenged to learn this skill/concept or lacks the prerequisite skills needed.	A student who is ready to learn this or is on grade level.	A student who is ready to move beyond this or is above grade level.
VISUAL	Use highlighters to color code similar initial consonants for words in a story.	Use highlighters to color code similar word chunks for words in a story.	Use chunking to read text with unfamiliar, higher-level vocabulary with a partner.
AUDITORY	Listen to a podcast on initial consonant sounds.	Listen to word rhymes and songs focused on families of words with similar word chunks in a listening center.	Create poems and songs focused on families of words with similar word chunks with a partner.
KINESTHETIC/TACTILE	Match pictures to initial consonant sounds.	Manipulate magnet strips with common word chunks to create words found in a story.	Use interactive white-board to manipulate word chunks and create new words in a small group.

Note: Readiness categories taken from Lev Vygotsky's work on the Zone of Proximal Development.

Appendix F
Dressing for the Temperature

How do we know what to wear? If it's 40° F outside, should you wear a coat or not? If it's 75° F, is it warm enough to put on a swimsuit? Create a guide for your family so they know what clothes are the best to wear at each temperature. Bring your guide home to put by your thermometer.

(Appendix F continues on next page.)

		Novice	Apprentice	Practitioner	Expert
Guidebook	Temperatures	♦ 4 different temperatures listed in correct degree format ♦ temperatures represent at least a 50-degree range	♦ 5 different temperatures listed in correct degree format ♦ temperatures represent at least a 50-degree range	♦ 6 different temperatures listed in correct degree format and in order from lowest to highest ♦ temperatures are separated by at least 10 degrees and represent at least a 70-degree range	all of *Practitioner* plus includes a temperature below zero
	Pictures of Clothing	♦ one picture for each temperature	♦ one picture for each temperature ♦ most pictures depict a person appropriately dressed for the temperature	♦ one picture for each temperature ♦ all pictures depict a person appropriately dressed for the temperature	all of *Practitioner* plus additional pictures included to account for different weather conditions (snow, rain, etc.) or different people in your family
	Format of Guidebook	♦ each page contains a temperature and picture	♦ cover page with name and relevant picture ♦ each page contains temperature and picture	♦ cover page with name and relevant picture ♦ each page contains temperature, picture, and one adjective describing that temperature	all of *Practitioner* plus each page contains a sentence about the picture that uses the adjective
Descriptions		student responds to oral prompts to describe temperature	student generally describes temperature independently	Student accurately describes temperature independently using several adjectives	all of *Practitioner* plus student identifies which seasons are most likely to contain that temperature

Appendix G
The Mozart Effect

Over the past two decades, studies have revealed that listening to music stimulates parts of the brain that otherwise never get used. The scientists conducting these studies have taken x-rays of the brain, and have "seen" that there is more activity while music is being played. An astounding piece of this research shows that while you listen to rock, rap, country, the blues, jazz, or classical, your brain tends to respond by adding different types of signals to its regular repertoire, as long as you're not so familiar with the particular musical composition that you're singing along.

Here's the clincher, though. The studies suggest that listening to Mozart has more of an effect than any other type of music. Mozart's music has a bigger effect than Mahler, Beethoven, Vivaldi, or that of any other classical artist. They have dubbed this the "Mozart Effect."

Perhaps you should recommend that your school play Mozart during the day in the hallways. But what about other music, perhaps from your personal favorite musical artists.? Before you make any recommendations, you'll need to know a little more about the "Mozart Effect."

The challenge before you is to explore Mozart and other classical composers along with Rock and Jazz artists in order to decide whether Mozart is the best for your brain, and *why*. You'll need to explore the music deeply, and focus on certain elements: tempo, key signatures, the combination of chords and their chordal construction, and even the instruments that are being played.

You will work in small groups to devise an explanation in the form of a proposal to the principal to explain why certain music should be played in the hallways during the change of class.

Good luck!

(Appendix G continues on next page.)

		Novice	Apprentice	Practitioner	Expert
Music Analysis	Mozart	writes a short paragraph for each of 6 of the elements listed under *Practitioner* for 1 musical composition	writes a short paragraph for each of the elements listed under *Practitioner* for 2 musical compositions	writes a short paragraph for each of 6 of the elements below in 3 musical compositions and compares and contrasts among compositions: ♦ meter ♦ tempo ♦ rhythm ♦ tonality ♦ intervals ♦ chords and/or chord progression ♦ harmony ♦ key signature	includes all 8 considerations listed under *Practitioner* plus explores tension and release in 2–3 of the compositions
	Other Classical Composer	writes a short paragraph for each of 6 of the elements listed under *Practitioner* for 1 musical composition	writes a short paragraph for each of the elements listed under *Practitioner* for 2 musical compositions and compares and contrasts the compositions	writes a short paragraph for each of the elements below in 2 musical compositions, compares and contrasts the 2 compositions and the works of Mozart and the other classical composer: ♦ meter ♦ tempo ♦ rhythm ♦ tonality ♦ intervals ♦ chords and/or chord progression ♦ harmony ♦ key signature	includes all 8 considerations listed under *Practitioner* plus explores tension and release in Mozart's work vs. that of the other classical composer

		Novice	Apprentice	Practitioner	Expert
Music Analysis	Choice: ☐ Rap ☐ Blues ☐ Jazz ☐ Rock ☐ House ☐ Baroque ☐ Other	writes a short paragraph for each of 6 of the elements listed under *Practitioner* for 1 musical composition in 1 genre	writes a short paragraph for each of the elements listed under *Practitioner* for 2 musical compositions by one artist	writes a short paragraph for each of the elements below in 2 musical compositions and compares and contrasts them with those of Mozart: ♦ meter ♦ tempo ♦ rhythm ♦ tonality ♦ intervals ♦ chords and/or chord progression ♦ harmony ♦ key signature	includes all 8 considerations under *Practitioner* plus explores how the genre is similar to and different from classical music
	Explanation of Effect on Brain Function	makes hypothesis based on above characteristics	♦ makes hypothesis based on above characteristics ♦ includes reference to 1 significant event in the performance	♦ makes hypothesis based on above characteristics ♦ includes reference to 2–3 significant events in the performance	all of *Practitioner* for 1–2 of Mozart's works and a comparison to the other composers
	Proposal to Principal	identifies the hypothesis	1–2 paragraphs identifying the hypothesis	♦ 1–2 paragraphs identifying the hypothesis as above ♦ explanation as to the elements of Mozart that might have a beneficial effect (or you may recommend another genre)	all of *Practitioner* plus recommendation for 2–3 selections by Mozart or other composer

Appendix H
Terrific Tours! Teacher Notes

This task will take place over the course of one or two weeks. Students will be learning about geography, history, and science related to one region of the United States. They will be using math skills to calculate travel times and plan a trip. Throughout the task, the teacher will need to provide benchmark lessons and *small-group mini-lessons* to help students build the concepts and skills they need to complete the task. Following are some tips for getting started with the task:

♦ Begin with a reflective activity. Bring in travel brochures. Have students work in pairs or threes to decide which brochures are the most enticing and why and which trips they might want to go on and why. After a specified period of time, facilitate a class discussion about the tours. Introduce the idea that they have started a company called *Terrific Tours* and that groups will be formed to be responsible for designing one of the company's soon-to-be-popular tours.

♦ Divide the class into groups of threes or fours (perhaps pairs if this is their first collaborative activity) and give them the task sheet. Ask each individual to read through the task sheet and rubrics and write down questions they have. Allow the groups to discuss and answer the questions. Then facilitate a class discussion on the remaining questions. If a group has an unanswered question, see if another student in the class can answer it. Answer only the questions that no one else can answer.

♦ Allow the groups to have some planning time to decide how they will go about the work. Let them fill out a schedule for what they will do next work session. Facilitate this so that each group and individual is planning to approach the task in a systematic and productive way.

♦ Develop the "State Fact Sheet" that includes all the information you want students to locate about each state in the region. This can be done by the teacher or through class discussion.

♦ Assign each group a region. This can be done by the teacher or through a process agreed upon by the class.

Terrific Tours!

Imagine if learning about the regions of the United States meant you could take a trip and actually visit all of the places you study. Anything is possible! Suppose you and your classmates created a company called *Terrific Tours*!

You are going to design a tour of a region of the United States. The trip should take two weeks by bus. You must drive through all of the states of the region and stop at points of historical significance, points of interest, and natural wonders. Design the trip, including the roads you will travel and the time schedule. Calculate driving time at an average of fifty miles per hour. Allow time for the stops along the way. Travel no more than ten hours a day. You will hand in the following:

- A map with the route highlighted;

- An index card for each stop with the description for the tour guide to read;

- An itinerary of times for each stop, numbers of miles between stops, and length of time at the stop; and

- A travel brochure with pictures of some of the tour stops to entice travelers to join you.

Assessment

Each group member will receive 25 points for his/her part of the above work. Additionally, the group will share a grade for the overall project and collaborative process.

Steps Along the Way

1. Become familiar with the region. Fill out a "fact sheet" on each state: name, date entered into the Union, country that originally explored the state, capital, important cities, natural resources, notable geographic highlights and the scientific explanation behind them, famous persons, and notable historic sites and their significance.

2. Draw and label a map of the region with highways, rivers, major cities, and mountains.

3. Decide upon the stops on your trip.

(Appendix H continues on next page.)

4. Plan the most efficient route to begin at one point and visit each stop.

5. Allocate times to be at each stop, calculating driving time at 50 mph. Create your itinerary.

6. Once you all agree upon the itinerary, highlight the route on your map.

7. Create an index card for each stop with the description for the tour guide to read.

8. Think of the overall trip. Brainstorm the highlights of the trip. Write ideas for persuading people to join the tour.

9. Identify pictures on the web that correspond to your region.

10. Design a threefold brochure for the trip.

Detailed Description of the Steps

♦ *Group planning session*—As a group, decide how you will go about the work. Determine the states that are in your region and divide the responsibility for researching each state among the members of the group.

♦ *Individual work*—Develop the "State Fact Sheet" that includes all the information you need to locate on your assigned state(s). Use a variety of resources. Each individual will receive a grade for this work.

♦ *Group planning session*—Share your information on each state. As a group, complete a regional chart of the information. Make sure that you learn the information for your region as you will be responsible for knowing the information on a quiz.

♦ *Group map*—Each student should pencil in the outline for his/ her state(s). Once all group members approve of location, scale, and outline, each student should outline the state in marker. Each student should then pencil in highways, rivers, cities, and mountains. Once approved by the group, each student should cover the pencil marks with marker. Individual students will be graded on their individual portion of the map.

♦ *Individual work*—Review the group information and research the region to develop a list of five to ten places to stop and why. Group planning session—Taking turns, each member should name one proposed stop and explain why it was chosen. The recorder should create a master list. The group should discuss each stop and the recorder should list the reactions. The group should then decide upon a list of stops to be included in the tour. Each member should mark the stops on his/her portion of the map. The group should divide the trip into sections

♦ *Individual work*—Each member should take a section and calculate the distances between stops and the time to travel between stops. This will become part of the itinerary.

♦ *Group planning session*—The group should discuss these times and plan a two-week trip, listing the travel times and stop times.

♦ *Individual work*—Each member should word processes the itinerary for his/her part of the trip w/ the approval of the group. You will be graded on your individual itinerary.

♦ *Individual work*—Each member should develop the index cards for his/her designated stops. You will be graded on your individual index cards.

♦ *Individual work*—Each member should review the entire trip, read all the cards, and brainstorm a list of reasons to take this tour. You will be given an individual quiz on your entire region.

♦ *Group planning session*—Discuss ideas and agree upon those to be presented in the brochure.

♦ *Individual work*—Search the Web for pictures, charts, maps, and information to be included in the brochure.

♦ *Group planning session*—Discuss a plan for the six panels (three front and three back) of the brochure and designate different members to design different panels.

♦ *Individual work*—Design panels and have a buddy from the group edit, revise, and comment on the work.

♦ *Group work*—Ensure that the brochure is uniform throughout, even though different panels were created by different people.

(Appendix H continues on next page.)

♦ *Group planning session*—Check rubrics to ensure that all components are completed to satisfaction. Have each member sign off on the project, signifying agreement that this is their best effort. Hand in the four components of the tour (map, brochure, index cards, itinerary).

Point-of-Interest Description — Index Cards

Your index cards will count as an individual assignment, worth a maximum of 25 points.

	somewhat (3 pts.)	mostly (4 pts.)	consistently (5 pts.)
neatly written in cursive			
written in complete sentences with no grammatical, punctuation, spelling, or capitalization errors			
use of descriptive words and phrases			
includes historical references and/or scientific explanation where appropriate			
includes obvious points as well as little-known information			

Point-of-Interest Description — Index Cards

Your index cards will count as an individual assignment, worth a maximum of 25 points.

	somewhat (3 pts.)	mostly (4 pts.)	consistently (5 pts.)
distances accurately calculated based on map key			
travel time accurately calculated based on an average speed of 50 mph			
time allotted per stop is based on the amount of sightseeing necessary			

tour time is planned for a total of 10 hours each day			
itinerary is laid out neatly in chart form with times for each of the stops and length of time for each stop			

Regional Map

Your work on your states on the map will count as an individual assignment, worth a maximum of 25 points.

	meets some of the specifications (3 pts.)	meets most of the specifications (4 pts.)	meets all of the specifications (5 pts.)
Accuracy/Neatness ♦ drawn to scale; detailed borders; all labels neatly printed; no spelling errors; coloring within the lines; route correctly and neatly highlighted			
Completeness ♦ includes all states in the region, capitals, other major cities, highways, rivers, and mountains; includes map key with symbols for all aspects, including historical and geographic sites			
Use of Color ♦ use of colors to match topography (rivers, oceans, plains, dessert, mountains, forests); optional shading of states does not interfere with above shading			
Information ♦ use of symbols and/or several text boxes around map to highlight points of interest			

(Appendix H continues on next page.)

Consistency ◆ map appears unified in spite of the fact that several members created it: coloring uniform; labeling uniform; symbols uniform			

Brochure

Your work on your panel(s) of the brochure will count as an individual assignment, worth a maximum of 25 points.

	meets some of the specifications (3 pts.)	meets most of the specifications (4 pts.)	meets all of the specifications (5 pts.)
Information ◆ includes necessary facts about the region and the tour; information presented in bullets and charts with limited amount of paragraph composition			
Persuasiveness ◆ paints a picture using descriptive words; use of pictures and/ or charts that "sell" the tour			
Layout ◆ mix of text and graphics; text and graphics do not overlap (unless as part of the design); whitespace used to separate components; use of different fonts and colors for different levels of information but not mixed within a level of text; graphics are appropriate to the message; panel is not overly busy or sparse; at least one-half-inch margin around edges			

Graphics ♦ uses photographs and/or clip art where appropriate			
Consistency of Look ♦ panel mixes well with the other panels in color; fonts; and over-all appearance			

Terrific Tours Group Assessment Rubric

This rubric will determine the group grade earned by the group in completing this project. This grade is in addition to the grades earned by individuals throughout the project.

	Novice (1)	Apprentice (2)	Practitioner (3)	Expert (4)	
Map, Index Cards, Itinerary, and Brochure	4 components are completed	4 components are somewhat uniform in presentation	4 components are uniform in presentation, making it hard to realize that more than one person completed them	all of *Practitioner* plus the 4 components follow an advertising theme	____ × 5 = ____
Technology		group uses technology for research, word processing, and brochure development with little required help	♦ group independently uses technology for research, word processing, and brochure development ♦ uses online collaboration	all of *Practitioner* plus creates an online, hyperlinked version of the brochure	____ × 4 = ____

(Appendix H continues on next page.)

	Novice (1)	Apprentice (2)	Practitioner (3)	Expert (4)	
Collaborative Planning	group usually allocates time for planning and group work when all members are present	group allocates time for planning and group work when all members are present; all members take part in all aspects of the work	◆ group allocates time for planning and group work when all members are present; all members take part in all aspects of the work; keeps log of items completed and to be completed	all of *Practitioner* plus uses Internet-based tools for scheduling and project management	___ × 4 = ___
Peer Assistance	members help one another when asked	members help one another by offering directions, feedback, and advice	◆ members help one another by offering both solicited and unsolicited directions, feedback, and advice ◆ members encourage one another	all of *Practitioner* plus members are careful to offer assistance that yields learning, rather than merely doing the other person's job	___ × 4 = ___
Conflicts	group addresses conflict by talking to the teacher	◆ group addresses conflict and reaches decisions through voting ◆ group members tend to bring issues to the teacher rather than one another	◆ group takes action to attempt to reach consensus but sometimes votes ◆ group members bring most issues to the table but involve the teacher at times	group works to reach consensus; members bring all issues to the table and deal with them	___ × 4 = ___

	Novice (1)	Apprentice (2)	Practitioner (3)	Expert (4)	
Scheduling	Some tasks are completed within deadlines	most tasks completed within deadlines or no less than one day late	all tasks completed within deadlines; group stays on schedule	all tasks are completed within deadlines; group stays on schedule and discusses challenges to assist in future planning	____ × 4 = ____

Appendix I
Learning Styles and Readiness Grid

When you stand before your class to teach a skill, you can be sure that students are not in the same place cognitively nor in terms of learning styles; consequently, instruction will be only moderately effective. Differentiated instruction involves using varied activities to meet the needs of all learners. Select a skill you might teach. Consider the student who already knows the skill you're about to teach, the student who is cognitively ready, and the student who lacks the prerequisite knowledge to learn the skill. Then, for each, consider three possible levels of learning styles. Brainstorm nine different ways a student could learn the same skill, preferably independent of the teacher. You may never have nine different activities going on at the same time for a skill, but you might choose, say, three.

SKILL:

	DISTAL ZONE A student who will be challenged to learn this skill/concept or lacks the prerequisite skills needed.	PROXIMAL ZONE A student who is ready to learn this or is on grade level.	CURRENT KNOWLEDGE A student who is ready to move beyond this or is above grade level.
VISUAL			
AUDITORY			
KINESTHETIC/TACTILE			

Note: Readiness categories taken from Lev Vygotsky's work on the Zone of Proximal Development.

Bibliography

Adams, J. (1990). *Conceptual blockbusting: A guide to better ideas* (3rd ed.). Reading, PA: Addison-Wesley.

Anderson, C. (2010, September 18). The web is dead. *Wired*, 118–127, 164.

Anderson, L., & Krathwohl, D. R. (2001). *A taxonomy for learning, teaching, and assessing—A revision of Bloom's taxonomy of educational objectives*. New York: Longman.

Barker, J. A. (1992). *Paradigms: The business of discovering the future*. New York: Harper Collins.

Carter, D. (2009, March 6). Podcast Trumps Lecture in One College Study. *eSchool News*. Retrieved from: http://www.eschoolnews.com.

Coleman, J. S. (1988). "Social capital in the creation of human capital." *American Journal of Sociology*, Supplement 94, S95–S120.

Csikszentmihalyi, M. (1990). *Flow: The psychology of optimal experience*. New York: Harper and Row.

de Bono, E. (1992). *Serious creativity*. New York: Harper Business.

de Bono, E. (1996). *Six thinking hats* (2nd ed.). Boston: Back Bay Books.

Eaker, R., DuFour, R., & DuFour, R. (2002). *Getting started: Reculturing schools to become professional learning communities*. Bloomington, IN: Solution Tree.

Festinger, L. (1957). A theory of cognitive dissonance. Evanston, IL: Row, Peterson.

Friedman T. (2006). *The world is flat*. London: Penguin.

Gardner, H. (2006). *Multiple intelligences: New horizons*. New York: Basic Books.

Gladwell, M. (2005). *Blink: The power of thinking without thinking*. New York: Little Brown and Company.

Glasser, W. (1998). *Choice theory: A new psychology of personal freedom*. New York: HarperCollins.

Hanifan, L. J. (1916). "The rural school community center." *Annals of the American Academy of Political and Social Science, 67*, 130–138.

Heifetz, R. A., & Linsky, M. (2002). *Leadership on the line: Staying alive through the dangers of leading*. Boston: Harvard Business School.

Hof, R. D. (2006, May 1). "My virtual life." *Business Week*, 72–82.

IDEportal. (2011). Retrieved from http://www.idepaortal.com.

Merriam-Webster Online Dictionary. (2010). "Infuse." Retrieved from http://www.merriam-webster.com/dictionary/infuse

Merriam-Webster Online Dictionary. (2010). "Integrate." Retrieved from http://www.merriam-webster.com/dictionary/integrate

Ophir, E., Nass, C., & Wagner, A. D. (2009). "Cognitive control in media multitaskers." *Proceedings of the National Academy of Sciences, 106,* 15583–15587.

Pink, D. (2006). *A whole new mind: Why right-brainers will rule the future.* New York: Penguin.

Plato. (1986). *Plato: Phaedrus* (C. J. Rowe, Trans.). Oakville, CT: Aris & Phillips.

Prensky, M. (2006). *Don't bother me mom: I'm learning!* St. Paul, MN: Paragon House.

Smith, F. (1998). *The book of learning and forgetting.* New York: Teachers College Press.

Sousa, D. (2003). *The Leadership Brain.* Thousand Oaks, CA: Corwin Press

Sousa, D. A. (2005). *How the brain learns.* (3rd ed.). Thousand Oaks, CA: Corwin Press.

Tapscott, D. (1998). *Growing up digital: The rise of the net generation.* New York: McGraw-Hill.

Tapscott, D. (2009). *Grown up digital: How the net generation is changing your world.* New York: McGraw-Hill.

Tapscott, D., & Williams, A. D. (2006). *Wikinomics: How mass collaboration changes everything.* New York: Penguin.

Toffler, A., & Toffler, H. (1980). *The third wave.* New York: Bantam.

Tomlinson, C.A. (1999). *The differentiated classroom.* Alexandria, VA: ASCD.

Vygotsky, L. S. (1978). *Mind and society: The development of higher psychological processes.* Cambridge, MA: Harvard University Press.

Wagner, T. (2008). *The global achievement gap.* New York: Basic Books.

Wiggins, W., & McTighe, J. (2005). *Understanding by design.* Alexandria, VA: ASCD.